Secret Signs, Symbols & Sigils

By Nigel Pennick

Secret Signs, Symbols & Sigils

Cover design by Daryth Bastin
Cover illustration by Nigel Pennick

Published by:

Capall Bann Publishing
Freshfields
Chieveley
Berks
RG20 8TF

Tel/Fax 01635 248711

Thanks and Credits

The author wishes to thank those people who have been helpful in various ways, both knowingly and unknowingly, in the gestation of this book: Michael Behrend, Julia Day, Jon Day, Nigel Jackson, K. Frank Jensen, Prudence Jones, Hans-Martin Kirschmann, Rosemarie Kirschmann, John Michell, the late Colin Murray, Les Randall, Ian Read, Jeff Saward, Jonas Trinkunas, Bob Trubshaw and Helen Woodley. Also the staffs of the Cambridge University Library and the Cambridgeshire Collection, both in the City of Cambridge.

Illustrations Credits:

Artwork by Nigel Pennick: Figs. Cover art, Frontispiece, 1, 2, 5, 6, 8, 9, 13, 14, 16, 18, 19, 20, 21, 24, 25, 26, 27, 28, 29, 30, 31, 35, 36, 37, 38, 39, 42, 43, 45, 46, 47, 48, 49, 50, 51, 52, 53 (valknut), 54.
Nideck Collection: 3, 4, 7, 10, 11, 12, 15, 17, 22, 23, 32, 33, 34, 40, 41, 44, 49, 53 (all except the valknut), 55.

Frontispiece: The Great Goddess, who simultaneously is an image of the human being, the earth spirit and the cosmos.

Contents

By the same author, also published by Capall Bann:

Runic Astrology
Inner Mysteries of the Goths
Sacred Geometry
Oracle of Geomancy
The Goddess Year (with Helen Field)
The New Celtic Oracle (with Nigel Jackson)

Introduction

This work is about the structure of the world, from the human perspective. Over the years, many people from both the religious and scientific outlook have attempted to demonstrate that it is possible to view existence from a point outside the human. However, as everyone who has claimed this has been human, it is difficult to understand how this myth of objectivity ever gained currency. We are ourselves, possessed of characteristics that are peculiar to the human condition, and it is through this character, unique on this planet at least, that we attempt to describe existence. As we perceive it, within the world there is a multiplicity of events, and it is only through our human senses and interpretative language that we are able to come to terms with the conditions within which we have our being. The human way of perception is through the symbols that we perceive either consciously or intuitively around and within us. Through these symbols, by comparison and combination, we can communicate with our fellow humans. Thus, to facilitate communication, our ancestors developed symbolic languages and alphabets that reflected in an inner way the outer phenomena of existence.

Symbolic ways of describing and understanding the world range from the conventions of language to myth and religion. In traditional society, the symbolic and the mythical are integrated with the activities of everyday life: there is no division between the physical necessities of existence and the deeper levels of the symbolic world. There, every thing, every activity, operates on a number of levels, each of which infuses and informs each other. Thus, in the traditional perception of materials, the physical nature of the stuff with which we must deal on the material level also expresses certain symbolic realities that are inherent in it; in turn, this is understood through an explanatory mythology, explained in poetic or narrative form. Such an integrated standpoint does not separate the physical from the spiritual or the human from the non-human. All is integrated, and an image of the wholeness that is existence. The symbolic world-view has ample space for many points of view, for the pluralism that allows new understanding to enter new situations, providing creative solutions to problems, and a world of multiple wonders.

Literalism, on the other hand, has shown itself to be a destructive blinkering of perception. Unfortunately for human culture, it is the easy, unconscious way of relating to the world, and so, sadly, it has become the dominant world-view in the 20th century. But, fortunately, also in this century, according to the Law of the Unity of Opposites, the antidote to this collective psychosis was offered to us by the perceptive psychologist Alfred Adler showed that "In literalism lies madness". Literalism, the belief that the symbolic description of the world is an actual reality in its own right, leads, on the spiritual side, to fundamentalistic behaviour, and in the material world to a forgetting of the implications of our actions. Once a symbol is taken literally, then battles can be fought over its meaning, and throughout history, human misery has been the result.

In keeping with the spirit of my earlier publications, this work is not one of literalism. It is not fundamentalistic. Rather, it is a Druidic exploration of the multiple ramifications of our human symbolic understanding of the world, from the perspective of Celtic civilisation, describing the symbolic structures upon which the more familiar symbols, sigils and signs of mainstream western spirituality, in the Graeco-Roman tradition, are based. Only by looking more deeply into the underlying structure of the traditional symbolic cosmos and understanding something of its nature, can we apply the ancient skills and wisdom of the past to the present day. The bitter fruits of literalism litter history, and it is up to those of us who can see through the falsity of literalism to repudiate them and to act accordingly with full consciousness. According to ancient Druidic ethics, the three principal endeavours are to learn, and collect knowledge; the second is to teach them; whilst the third is to make peace, and to put an end to all injury. To carry out the third endeavour is the objective of the previous two. This book is offered to the reader in this spirit "For to do contrary to these things is not usual or becoming to a Bard."

NIGEL CAMPBELL PENNICK, Bar Hill, Midsummer 1995 C.E.

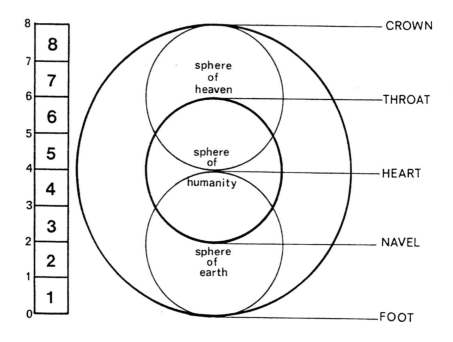

Chapter 1

The Human Body

According to the earliest recorded spiritual understanding of the human being's place in the scheme of things, in our constitution, each of us is a reflection of the cosmos. This is expressed best in the maxim ascribed to Hermes Trismegistus, founder of alchemy, "As above, So below". In another, fuller, form, recorded in the *Tabula Smaragdina* (*The Emerald Table of Hermes Trismegistus*), the maxim is rendered "That which exists in the greater world (the macrocosmos) is reflected perfectly in the lesser world (the microcosmos)", so that the wonders of the One are enacted. The macrocosm, the greater world, is the cosmos at large, or (to those who believe in the universe theory), the universe; whilst the lesser world is the human being. This works on two levels. Because human consciousness is for us the only measure of existence, we can come to terms only with those elements of the cosmos that are reflected in human experience. This experience, in turn, is

---

Fig. 1. This diagram illustrates the symbolic spiritual link between the human being, space and number. Geometrically, it has eight sections that reflect, among other things, the ogdoad, the eightfold nature of existence perceived by the ancient Egyptian sages, the archaic Indo-European eight-day week and the Ostyak shaman's cosmic axis pillar of 7 notches. The upright human being forms the link between the heavens above and the earth below. A related concept that shows the body as unifying that which is below and that which is above can be seen in the illustration of the Great God Pan (fig. 40).

related totally to our physical and mental constitution. Thus it is that certain aspects of existence can be described in terms of the human body and its experiences.

Until the rise of modern science in the eighteenth century, every branch of philosophy and religion acknowledged this relationship of the human to the cosmos. It is the fundamental principle that underlay traditional medicine, alchemy, magic and religion. Although thoroughly Pagan in origin, the 'Church Father', Augustine of Hippo, acknowledged this Hermetic tradition, and incorporated it into Christian orthodoxy when he wrote: "God therefore placed on the earth the man whom He made, as it were another world, the great and large world in the small and little world". Following Augustine, Gregory Nazianzene stated; "Every creature, both heaven and earth, are in man", and Zanchius, in his *De Opera Dei* (*On the Works of God)*, asserts "The body of man is the image of the world, and called therefore *microcosmus*". To the Welsh Bard, Taliesin, are attributed two poems *Canu y Byd mawr* (*The Great World*), and *Cany y Byd bychan* (*The Little World)*. They are the Celtic manifestations of the Hermetic Maxim. "I came from the Great World" says the Bard to his disciple, "having my beginning in Annwn". "I am in the Little World....and now I am a man...". A millennium later, in his *Occult Philosophy*, the German magus Heinrich Cornelius Agrippa von Nettesheim (1486 - 1535), explained, "God also created Man after His own image; for as the world is an image of God, so Man is the image of the world". In the same period, the revered Welsh bard Iorwerth Vynglwyd (1460 - 1500) wrote: "Saith the revered Bardism, A little world is man in his vigour, under the light."

According to the Bardic cosmological teachings of Welsh Druidism, which are the unbroken continuation of the Hermetic tradition of the west, each of the elements of existence is reflected in the constitution of the human being. As part of the *Philosophia Perennis*, Bardic descriptions often contain aspects found in Christian theology, for, as all religions emanate from within the human psyche as interpretations of the unchanging facts of existence, so, at the deepest level, they arise from the same roots and contain the same core. Bardic teachings are progressive: first they describe the elements that compose the cosmos; then they demonstrate the relationship between the cosmos, the human being and the divine.

The Bardic text, *Trioedd Barddas, A Elwir Trioedd Ionabwy* (*The Triads of Bardism, Called the Triads of Ionabwy*) contains a passage *Yr Elfyddennau* (*The Elements*), which describes the symbolic structure of existence: "There are three original principles, which are the three primary elements: the first, calas, hence all hardness, as it hardens every other thing that comes into contact with it, and from this comes all physical structure; the second, water [fluidity], and hence all freshness and softness, and it freshens and softens everything which is mixed with it, and all moisture and physical change; the third, *nwyvre*, and hence all life, for whatever it mixes with becomes alive, as far as its species and capability permit."

"Other teachers and wise men" quoted in *Barddas* taught that there are five elements: *calas*, water, ; air fire and *nwyvre*. It appears that the three element system is the older of the two, being in keeping with the triadic view of existence of ancient Celtic spirituality. It seems that the later Bardic tradition was able to create a synthesis of the threefold Celtic system and the Four Elements of Hermetic symbolic cosmology. Thus, the standard Bardic teaching was encapsulated in the text: "There are five elements: earth, which is *calas*; fluidity, which is water and freshness; air, and hence all breathing, every voice and speech; fire, and hence all heat and light; and nwyvre, whence proceeds all life, intelligence, knowledge, and power from will and desire."

According to *Trioedd Doethineb* (*The Triads of Wisdom*), "Manred, the original form of all the materials, or all the consitutuents, that is, the elements, of which the first four of the five were lifeless, namely, calas, fluidity, breath and fire, until God animated them by uttering His Name, when instantly they became alive in one triumphant song, and manifested their condition." *Nwyvre,* which in contemporary Pagan thought is viewed as an independent 'force', here is symbolised as a manifestation of the Creator. "It is in *nwyvre* that God exists", another text tells us, "as well as every soul, which is also from Him". Similarly, in John Bradford's Bardic book, *Brith Y Coed,* the text, *Wythh Defnydd Dyn (The Eight Materials of Man)* demonstrates the unity of the human with the divine:

"1. From the earth is the flesh; 2. from the water, the blood; 3. from the air, the breath; 4. from the calas [hardness - N.P.], the bones; 5. from the salt, his feeling; 6. from the sun, or fire, his agitation [motion - N.P.]; 7. from the truth, his understanding; 8. from the Holy Ghost [Yspryd Glân], that is, God, his soul or life."

Also, the Bardic text titled *Athronddysg Y Bardd Glas O'r Gadair (The Philosophy of the Blue Bard of the Chair)* relates the parts of the human body to our powers and emotions:

"In the forehead is the intellect;
In the nape is the memory
In the pate is discretion;
In the understanding, memory, and discretion together, is reason;
In the lungs is the breath;
In the breast is lust;
In the liver is the heat;
In the veins is the blood;
In the bile is anger;
In the spleen is joyousness;
In the heart is love;
In all these is affection;
In the affection is the soul;
In the soul is the mind;
In the mind is faith;
In faith is the Son of God;
In the Son of God is imperishable life;

In imperishable life is gwynvyd without end.

And blessed is he, who rightly exercises the faculties with which God has endowed him, in order to attain Gwynvyd, for ever and ever. Amen. The Blue Bard of the Chair has said it!"

On another level, this system of correspondences reflects the inner workings of time and space as perceived symbolically. Thus, for example, the types of experience categorised as the signs of the zodiac are reflected in certain parts of the human body; likewise, aspects of landscape reflect certain human characteristics; similar correspondences may be found in the mineral, plant and animal kingdoms. All humane architecture which relates to people as living beings reflects certain aspects of the human body. Exoterically, this is manifested in the structure of the building, whilst esoterically, it is inherent in the measurements and proportions that all architects who still follow the canons of tradition use as the ruling principles of their structures. In this, quoting the maxim of the Greek philosopher Protagoras (6th century BCE) "Man is the measure of all things; of being things that they exist, and of nonentities that they do not exist".

The rulership of the zodiac figures to the human body is a fundamental part of European traditional esoteric lore. According to this system, which may have been formalised in ancient Babylon, the head, including the senses of vision and hearing, is ruled by the powers of Aries, whilst the neck, throat and voice is under the regency of the powers of Taurus. The two arms and hands are ruled by the twins, Gemini, whilst Cancer rules the breasts and lungs, and Leo the heart Virgo is linked with the bowels, whilst Libra controls the kidneys and the Solar Plexus. The genitalia are under the rulership of the sign of the Scorpion, whilst the muscular powers of Sagittarius are reflected in the thighs. The knees are ruled by Capricorn, whilst the lower legs are under the power of Aquarius and the feet, whose prints resemble fish, Pisces. The traditional ascription of rulerships of the parts of the body to their

9

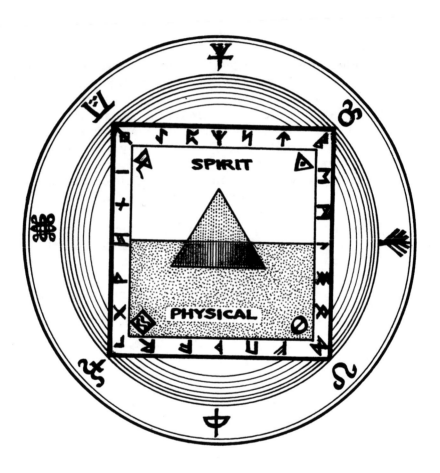

corresponding zodiacal powers demonstrates perfectly the Hermetic maxim. Taken as a form of traditional taxonomy, this system of correspondences is a manifestation of the traditional way of thinking that is at once descriptive and symbolic, holding within each aspect of itself great meaning. Similarly, the different parts and aspects of the human body may be classified according to the qualities and virtues of other mantic systems, such as the individual runes or the sixteen figures of divinatory geomancy. (For details of this, see the author's The *Oracle of Geomancy*, Capall Bann, 1995).

This reflection of the human body in the heavens above is found equally in the earth below. Certain forms of the human body are often perceptible as landscape features. In Ireland, for instance, hills such as The Paps of Anu in Ireland are named as the breasts of the local earth goddess. Human structures are inherent in the very names of landscape features, for instance coastal 'necks of land' and 'headlands' reflects a human view of terrestrial structures. There are many other instances of this, for it is a general principle. A full description of the anthropomorphic aspects of the landscape in the Celtic tradition can be found in the author's book, *Celtic Sacred Landscapes* (Thames and Hudson, 1996).

In the west, bodily activity in the shape of the martial arts, too, has a significant esoteric dimension. The relationship between the proportions of the body and fighting styles is implicit in ancient Greek representations of combat. In the Renaissance, the application of the esoteric geometrical proportions of the human body to the martial arts led to a great leap forward in technique. Sixteenth-century works on sword-fighting by the Italian philosopher-mathematician and architect Camillo

---

Fig. 2. This diagram shows the cosmos as conceived in the English Elven System of spirituality, related to the circle of runes, the four elements, the four directions and the eight festivals of the year.

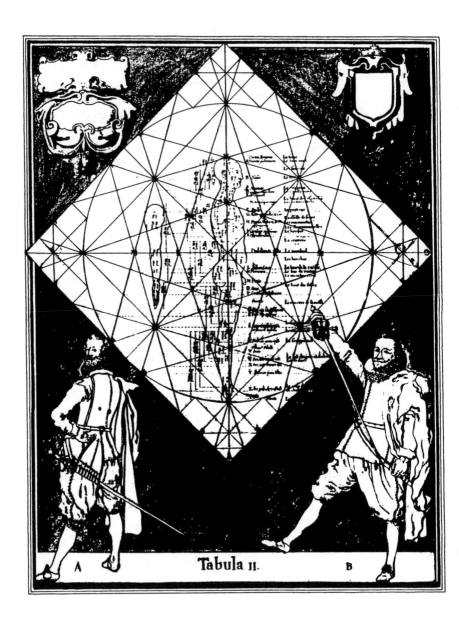

Tabula II.

Agrippa and the Spanish masters Jeronimo Carranza and Luis Panchero refined the art according to mystical principles. The greatest esoteric master of fencing, however, was Gerard Thibault, who, having studied the art according to classical occult principles, defeated all of the acknowledged masters in public competition.

Thibault's book, *L'Académie de L'Espée* (1628), which took fifteen years to produce, explained how the human body is a microcosm of the cosmos: "Man is the most perfect and most excellent of all the world's creatures. In him one can see, among other indications of divine wisdom, in his wholeness and his principal parts such an exquisite reflection of the whole universe that he has rightly been named by the ancient philosophers *Microcosm*, that is to say "the little world". For, excepting the dignity of his soul, which is extremely superior to all perishable things, his body comprises the epitome, not only of everything that one sees here on earth, but also all that is in heaven itself, reproducing everything with such a gentle harmony, beautiful and complete, and with such a precise correspondence in number, measure and weight, that it is related miraculously to the virtues of the four elements and the influences of the planets, so that there is nothing like it to be found in any other place."

When one fights according to the inner principles that underlie the structure and movement of the human body, then the principles of the divine harmony will ensure that all is in order. In Thibault's system, the swordsman uses a rapier of a size

---

Fig. 3. Diagram by Gerard Thibault, (1628) showing the geometry of the human body as related to the martial art of sword-fighting. The spiritual geometry of the human body, taught by the Pagan philosophers of antiquity according to the Hermetic Maxim, "As above, so below", is related by master swordsman Thibault directly to the moves of fencing, which themselves reflect and use the powers of the four elements and the virtues of the seven astrological planets.

perfectly related to his bodily geometry, and fights on ground upon which conceptual geometrical patterns are projected. The important aspect of Gerard Thibault's principles is that they were verified in the merciless testing-ground of combat, and proved to be the best way to win. Similar principles were used by the famed French occultist and swordsman Cyrano de Bergerac. The principles were transmitted to the other great western martial art, boxing, by the fencer, cudgel-fighter and boxer, James Figg, acknowledged in 1719 as the first British heavyweight boxing champion. Developed by Jack Broughton, who in 1734 formulated the first rules of boxing, the art was perfected by the champion of England, Daniel Mendoza, in 1794. Thus the western martial art of boxing, finally formalised by the Marquess of Queensberry, is a contemporary manifestation of the sporting traditions of the ancient world, based ultimately upon the spiritual principles that link the individual human with the cosmos.

Because we perceive every aspect of existence through our senses and technological extensions of them, it is clear that those abstract ideas perceived as the 'laws' of Nature are also extensions or projections of the human being. Frequently, scientists and priests assert that their favoured hypotheses are in some way eternal and immutable 'laws', rather than more or less rational speculations based on tradition, observation and deduction. Those who regard these viewpoints as 'laws' that have some truth outside the human realm inevitably leads to conflict between protagonists of differing hypotheses who almost invariably regard other suggestions to be in opposition to their own views. Suspending consciousness, they promote their own views as objective truth, whilst disparaging the others as erroneous. This dualistic attitude tends to elevate

---

Fig. 4. Daniel Mendoza, the boxing champion of England, who, in the classical western tradition, in 1794 revolutionized the technique of the most basic of the European martial arts whilst maintaining the spirit of earlier times.

hypothesis to dogma, thence to orthodoxy, which is hypothesis transformed to spectacle. Then, the last resort of this is to defend the position with violence: it may even go on the offensive, and persecute others who do not agree.

But all of this is unnecessary. Those who build up systems of inflexible orthodoxy fail to recognise that essentially all knowledge is incomplete, that the cosmos is pluralistic, and that all things have a built-in failure rate. These 'laws of Nature' are best viewed as hypotheses that enable us to deal with the phenomena in limited and circumscribed circumstances: essentially, they are in continuous flux, acting pluralistically on many levels simultaneously. In his *Meditations*, the Stoic Emperor Marcus Aurelius (121 - 180 CE) wrote: "One thing rushes into existence, another rushes out of it. Even at the moment when something is in the process of coming into being, some part of it has already ceased to exist. The fabric of the cosmos is always being renewed by flow and change, even as the unceasing flow of time continually renews the appearance of eternity. In such a flowing river, in which there is no firm foothold, what can one value among the various things that are speeding past? It would be similar to setting ones affections on some sparrow flying past, which in the same instant is lost to the sight."

Also, the perceived correspondences that lie at the fundamentals of language and hence the human perception of existence, are often dismissed by literalists as fanciful or stupid. Of course, only a literalist would, for example, claim that a breast-shaped hill is actually *the* breast of Mother Earth, and act accordingly. Similarly, believing that a hand-shaped cloud is *actually* God's finger pointing out the sins of humankind is no more than literalistic fantasy. However, when taken symbolically, they may help us to recognise the larger world within which we exist. But when the symbolic sides of these resemblances are dismissed as meaningless, then the other side of literalism also goes too far. The ability to perceive a feature or event that resembles something else is a

16

fundamental quality of being human, and those who dismiss it as meaningless ultimately devalue our inner natures towards meaninglessness. Once that has occurred, the cosmos is denatured and devalued in our eyes, which are the only eyes through which we can perceive existence.

Chapter 2

Human Existence, the Cosmos and the Ensouled World

The Greek word Cosmos means the right placing of the multiple things of the world. It is the aesthetic, polyvalent, polytheistic arrangement of the things of existence. The right orderliness of things, so that all things work in harmony - the divine harmony. The maxim of the Great Goddess, *Ordo Ab Chao* (order out of chaos), expressed in modern terminology, is that the cosmos is a self-ordering system, which, in a state of balance, has produced life and consciousness. The spiritual conception of Cosmos is far more than the narrow, reductionist view of 'Universe', which comes from the words *Unus-versus*, meaning 'everything circling around one point', or, by reduction 'turned into one'. When we use the word Universe to describe being, then the actual concept we are using denies the essential plurality of existence. 'Universe' is essentially dualistic, where being is presented as existing in opposition to chaos, which is perceived as disorder, displacement and derangement. But, as recent developments in Chaos Mathematics have shown, order arises out of chaos, not through some mysterious opposition to it.

The human being's place in the cosmos, both in space and time, is related largely to the structure of our bodies. Physically, we are bilaterally symmetrical beings, with a front and a back, a left and a right side, and, naturally, we envisage the world in terms of these directions. Whether or not we recognise this perception consciously, it is innate in our constitution. It affects fundamentally our interpretation of the nature of reality. Every human expression and artifact is related ultimately to this structure. Mythically, the natural division of the perceived field around our bodies is displayed in the concept as the human body as the temple of the Gods.

In the Northern Tradition, this appears in the myth of the androgynous primal giant Ymir, whose body is dismembered and distributed to form the archetypal world. This perception underlies classical western occultism, as expressed in the Hermetic Maxim, "As above, so below", which denotes the correspondences between the outer world of external existence and the inner world of the human consciousness. Because our whole experience of reality comes only through our senses, our understanding of the world is coloured through-and-through with this structural reality. It is this reality that runs through human culture. Writing and symbols, art and architecture, technology and warfare are all structured according to the nature and needs of the human body.

The fourfold division of the world, and its further subdivision into the eight directions known as airts is derived directly from the structure of the human body and its interaction with the physical structure and processes of the planet upon which we evolved and upon which we live. At the centre of this fourfold division is the individual person, the source, fount and origin, the navel, the relic of the point from which each of us developed as an embryo within our mother.

Navel-points in the landscape are known in geomantic terminology by its Greek name of *omphalos*. This terminology, calling the central point a navel, reiterates the slain giant motif of the primal creation of the world, where each part of the human being is reflected in its corresponding structure in the world. In human beings, the navel is the vestige of the umbilical cord which once connected the unborn baby to the placenta in the mother's womb. Through the *omphalos*, the

20

material world is linked by a cosmic axis upwards to the creative, generative upperworld and downward to its complementary opposite, the degenerative or destructive underworld.

This pattern of a centre in this world linked by an axis to the upperworld above and the netherworld below is the basis for traditional sacred cosmology. It exists throughout the world in different cultural contexts. In central and northern Europe, the religious systems of the Celtic, Germanic and Baltic peoples are so structured. Traditional physical artifacts of the geomantic layout of the countryside and urban settlements naturally reflect this cosmic axis. It is the stable structure of society without which there is disorder and disintegration.

The determination of such a powerful cosmic centre, so vitally important in psychological as well as social terms, was one of the major tasks of the augur or locator, the geomants of old Europe, and many folk-tales recall these arduous quests. As the individual's spirit is centred in the physical body, and that body must have a location in space, so the local *anima loci* was perceived at a specific place - the local *omphalos* or navel. Just as the individual's spirit can be seen as being simultaneously separate and part of the divine spark, so the local spirit of place is at once separate as the local centre, and identical with the primal central point. Such is the mystery of the relationship between microcosm and macrocosm, "As above, so below". The central navel of the earth, symbolically represents the fixed point at which other states of consciousness and spiritual evolution may be attained by those attuned to such things by dint of personal effort or divine designation.

Fig. 5. The mounted dragonslayer whose lance performs the geomantiuc act, creating an image of the upright cosmic axis that links earth and heaven (after Albrecht Dürer).

The discovery of such a place of symbolic power, its definition and the geomantic act is enshrined in the mythos of dragonslaying in the stories of such luminaries as the Pagan heroes Cadmus, Siegfried and Beowulf, and in Christian mythology, Saints such as Beatus, George, Leonard, Martha and Michael and knights like Lord Lambton. Each dragon-slaying legend has a general or specific location and appropriate associated tales that attest to the stories' veracity. In each of these legends, the dragon, wyrm or serpent that is killed is often taken to symbolise the earth energies which, sensitive people assert, roam, bewilderingly and dangerously free in the soil and the underlying rock formations beneath our feet. In traditional society, the determination of the most powerful and appropriate location for the fixation of these energies (and there appears to be some leeway within an area of several square yards), was the task of the locator. After long and meticulous scrutiny of the site, would decide upon the correct time to undertake the geomantic act.

According to geomantic symbolism, at a designated instant, when the forces were at their most malleable, and when the energies could be best tamed, the locator would drive a peg or staff, or perhaps a lance or sword into the earth as the culmination of the foundation ceremony. Factors to be taken into account in determining the best time for the geomantic act were numerous. They depended upon local custom, the principles of electional astrology and other, more esoteric methods. All would be applied with the greatest care to ensure the efficacy of the geomantic act, for it can only be done once, and a mistake is permanent. Piercing of the ground at the optimal location appears to fix these wandering energies permanently in an accessible place. Some dowsers claim that such places are invariably blind springs. In dowsing terminology, a blind spring is a place where underground water rises towards the surface as it would at a spring. But, instead of emerging from the earth as a water flow, the water moves off somewhere else underground. But to a dowser, the effect of a blind spring upon the divining rods is similar to that produced by a spring, and this is why such a place is commonly called a place of power.

Incidentally, it is possible that the performance of the geomantic act at an appropriate place have the effect of creating a virtual blind spring for a rhabdomant or dowser. Whatever the ins-and-outs of western geomantic technique, and there are many 'schools', every dragonslaying myth presents the outcome of the act as the triumph of order over chaos - the imposition of human order upon random - and dangerous - nature. Often, the act is performed as a kind of self-defence in response to something destructive of human life. The classical St George myth is one of these. Sometimes, as in the Northumbrian legend of the Lambton Worm, the disruption produced by the unbridled energies are the result of human interference, but more generally, the dragonlike forces had arisen spontaneously necessitating a drastic remedy.

Many depictions of the geomantic act show the hero or heroine transfixing the dragon with a stave, sword or spear, which frequently runs through the head to pin it to the ground below. For instance, the medieval font in the church at Avebury in Wiltshire shows this, with a Bishop's crozier despatching the reptile. Paolo Uccello's celebrated painting in the National Gallery in London, in which the dragon is being knackered by a mounted St George shows it tethered lightly on a leash by the virgin whom the knight is ostensibly rescuing from its clutches. The nailing of the dragon's head reflects the important Western mystery of the Pendragon (dragon's head).

This mystical concept is found in many places, most notably in the epithet of King Arthur's father, Uther Pendragon, high king of Britain. In Northern Tradition spiritual symbolic kingship, the strength and health of the monarch, as head of the nation, is indistinguishable from that of the land. When he or she is strong and worthy, the land flourishes in unity, peace, fruitfulness and prosperity. When he or she is weak or unworthy, the land disintegrates in crime, factionalism, greed

and poverty. Also, once these magical aspects of kingship are no longer recognised, disintegration occurs.

The medieval legend of the Wasting of the Land of Logres is connected directly with the destruction wrought by an unworthy king who only cares for self-aggrandisement and the accumulation of wealth for the satisfaction of personal greed, which, when emulated by his courtiers and knights, leads inevitably to the downfall of the country.

Symbolically, King Arthur's withdrawal of the sword from the stone to assert his right of kingship of Britain, is a reversal of the geomantic act. In removing the sword, Arthur frees the dragon power which, as Pendragon himself, the king can control. It appears to be no coincidence that Arthur's military successes against the Saxon invader were in mobile cavalry warfare, not in static and centred defence. The withdrawal of the sword was concomitant with Arthur's digging-up of the head of Bendigaidvrân (Bran the Blessed), from Bryn Gwyn. In English, this hill is called the White Mount. From time immemorial it was the holy hill of the City of London, upon which Gundulph's White Tower of the Tower of London now stands. The miraculous head of Bendigaidvrân was symbolically the foundation sacrifice of Britain, a magic talisman planted in a place where its magical power would protect forever the island of Britain from conquest by an enemy. Arthur, believing in his own personal power, perhaps empowered also by Christian belief, removed the head, thus ultimately allowing the creation of England by invaders and

---

Fig. 6. "Wie Oben, so Unten", 'As above, So below", expressed according to the Ariosophical runic system which has been influential in Germany in the 20th century. The eighteen runes taught by the Austrian mystic Guido von List circle the archetypal triskele which divides the circle into three sections, representing respectively the World of the Highest; the World of the Equally High; and the World of the Third, the three beings who, in *Gylfagynning* give Gylfi knowledge of the history and structure of the existence.

immigrants from what is now Denmark, Germany and Holland. These acts took place at the time of the wasting of the land of Logres, and indicate the historic breakdown of formal geomancy and static, centralised, government at that time.

The symbolic binding or immobilisation of the dragon, perhaps prior to pinning it down (as in the light leash of Uccello's masterpiece) is paralleled by several myths of the binding or attempted restraint of other demonic beings, including the Norse Fenris-Wolf, Loki, and the World Serpent Jörmungand. In Celtic tradition, lake monsters like the Addanc and the River Ness beastie banished by St Columba parallel the casting-down of Satan, in Judaeo-Christian eschatology. Most of these beastly beings are overcome by gods or heroes, bound, and cast down into the underworld, where their periodic writhing in the torment of their bondage occasions earthquakes. In the landscape, the connection between the bound demon and tectonic tremors, and the location, *inter alia* of a key Swiss dragonslaying legend at a cave on a major alpine fault near Interlaken at St Beatushöhle, demonstrates some considerable intuitive geological acumen in antiquity, practised by those knowledgeable in the craft of location.

The World Serpent Jörmungand, lying along the ocean bed appears to be an ancient skaldic kenning that describes the deep mid-oceanic ridges. When these ridges shift with the movements of the tectonic plates of the world, they quake occasionally, vibrating the Bones of the Earth and generating tidal waves in the ocean like some awesome leviathan of the deep. Through all this cataclysmic displacement, the cosmic axis alone remains unshaken, being possessed of the immobility and permanence not possessed even by the Earth herself.

Chapter 3

The Cosmic Axis

Traditions concerning the cosmic axis itself have come down to us from Pagan antiquity, through the Germanic and Norse descriptions of the sacred pillar Irminsul, the tree of life, Yggdrassill, and in the sacred cosmology of the Celtic *Barddas*. The Saxon tradition is preserved for us in the accounts of the destruction by Christian zealots of the sacred pole Irminsul, which was symbolic of the sustaining power of the sky god who has many names, Irmin, Zeus, Deus, Jupiter, Ziu, Tîwaz, Tîw, Tyr, Termagant, etc. This great symbol of Heathen piety which stood at the Eresburg, now Ober-Marsberg in Westphalia, Germany, was extirpated cruelly by the Emperor Charles the Great in the year 772 c.e., during his cultural genocide of the Pagan Saxons. But its form survives in the Romanesque carvings at the Externsteine nearby to the town of Horn. If this image is to be taken literally, Irminsul was a representation of a palm tree, resembling closely the Babylonian tree of life.

The related Nordic world-tree Yggdrassill is better documented, as the Pagan faith continued and developed in Scandinavia until well after the year 1100 c.e. Unlike the physical Irminsul, which was ultimately destroyed by religious fundamentalists, Yggdrassill is not of this world. It is described in the Norse story *Gylfagynning (The Deluding of Gylfi)*, as follows: "The Ash is the best and greatest of trees; its branches spread out over the whole world to reach out over heaven...". This cosmic tree contains all things, linking the spring of Urd, the primal fountain of life and wisdom, at its roots, with the abode of the

Gods above. In its branches are the manifold manifestations of human existence. This unchanging vertical axis is the upright stave that is the essential feature of each character in the runic 'alphabet'.

The ancient British tradition taught by the Druids is the most coherent exposition of this system. It was almost lost at one time, but fortunately it was pieced together again from ancient manuscripts saved from Rhaglan Castle by the great Welsh bard Llewellyn Sion of Glamorgan (c.1560-1616). In the Bardic tradition, there are four linked 'circles of being' (*Y cylchau*), which can be viewed as being stacked, one above the other, around the cosmic axis. In effect, only three *cylchau* are accessible by humans, for the uppermost, Ceugant, is the unreachable sole abode of the transcendent creator, Hên Ddihenydd, the ineffable divine principle of being to whom all religions ultimately address themselves, whether they know it or not. In the late Nordic tradition, this supreme deity is identified with the Allfather Odin. At some point, Odin superseded either Thor or Tyr as the chief god, though in Norway, Thor remained the most popular. Here, in Odinic symbolism, Ceugant is an exact parallel of the Air Throne, Hliχskjálf, which is the seat accessible only to the High One and his consort, Frigg. From Hliχskjálf, the Allfather or the Queen of Heaven can view the nine worlds of Norse cosmology.

Fig. 7. Our Lady, from a 17th century Roman Catholic devotional print. She is depicted as the Queen of Heaven, standing on the moon, crowned by stars and with sun and moon in attendance. Like her apparitions, in which the otherworldly power we call Our Lady appears in human form, she floats above the enclosed garden, before which is a fountain in the form of the cosmic axis, flanked by trees of life, a cypress and a palm tree. The form of the palm reflects the water of the fountain. It is this image that appears in the Germanic cosmic axis, Irminsul, rune-stones, and the Romani alphabet character *faí*. The well to the right gives access to the underworld.

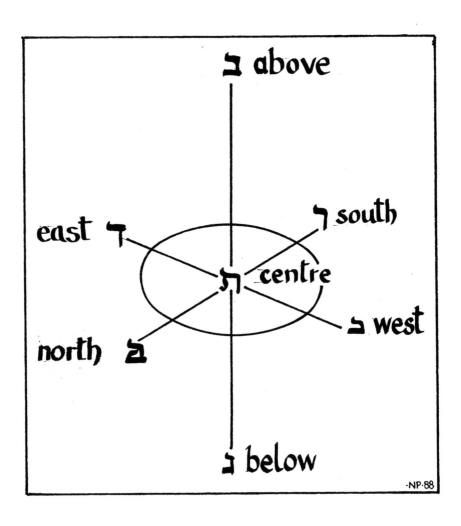

ב above

east ד

ר south

ה centre

ב west

north ב

ב below

-NP·88

In British Bardism, the *cylch* (circle) immediately below Ceugant is Gwynvyd, the White Land, whose name signifies the quality of Felicity. This is the abode of the enlightened: the goddesses and gods and people who have transcended the reincarnatory cycle of their Earthly lives. Below this is the middleworld, Abred, upon which we are born as human being, live, experience joy and sorrows, reproduce and die. The Bardic name Abred also has the alternative kenning of Adfant, which means The Place with the Turned-Back Rim, an allusion to the 'flat Earth' concept. In Abred, good and evil equipreponderate, and hence here there is free will for all.

In Abred every conscious act is one of consent or choice. Whatever one does, one always has an alternative possibility to do it do differently, and therefore it is appropriate that one should receive punishment or reward according to one's acts or works. In actuality, there is no external enforcer of the 'reward' or 'punishment', rather these words describe the inevitable consequences of any wilful act. Acting also upon Abred is the force or process whose common English description, destiny, does not depict it adequately. The Saxon word Wyrd or the Norse örlog is better, for it includes all of the forces, events, accidents and ideas which have made now what it is, but is not determinate. In Abred, we cannot avoid our örlog, but our actions with regard to it are vitally important. In the worst case, our örlog may make it impossible for us to do right, trapping us within a narrow choice-field from which our actions must produce ill effects no matter what we do. Then, the 'creative Pagan acceptance of life', as Eugene O'Neill put it, is our Wyrd here.

Fig. 8. According to Qabalistic beliefs, the seven 'double letters' of the Hebrew alphabet each have their place in the seven directions of space, which are the axes and points of the human body, manifested in human consciousness.

In Peter Bruegel's famous painting *De Tolle Gret* (*Mad Meg*), which shows a witch, the Bardic cosmology is depicted in the background as a typical tree of the trained linden type one encounters as a *Dorflinde* in parts of Germany and the Netherlands. Here, on the Abred level, figures are shown in dance or combat. On one side, a horned being, in medieval symbolism emblematical of evil or wrong action personified as the Devil, grapples with a human figure. On the other side (the right, customarily the side of good) a musician plays the Krummhorn. Seemingly, and appropriately, this figure opposes the horned being's demonic advances. In a painting made as late as 1564, it is difficult to decipher the precise attributes of the characters, but the triple-tiered arrangement of the tree, and the cage beneath it, emblematical of the abyssal underworld, Annwn, is apparent.

Bardic tradition asserts that in Abred, human beings undergo successive reincarnations. This is reflected in the ancient Cornish saying, "Ni fuil an sabras athragad death", There is nothing in death but an alteration of life. Here, in Abred, the spirit lives a series of lives in the physical body in free will, with spiritual progression or retrogression dependent on the actions taken. The perpetration of real evil, such as the wanton destruction of life, ends in a fall down the cosmic axis into the abyss of Annwn, the Loveless Place or Land Invisible. This fall is called obryn, that is, transmigration into a lower form. However Annwn cannot be equated with the Christian doctrine of Hell, for the Druidic Annwn is not in any way God's concentration camp, but is a dynamic, growing state that contains lower insensate matter and organisms that have not developed or progressed sufficiently yet to enter Abred. Here, in Breugel's painting, the beings are caged, and the bars exactly parallel the supports we can see today on many a Dorflinde, where the lower branches are supported by wooden or even stone pillars. Unlike the Christian Hell, which is an irreversible and eternal torture-chamber, Annwn releases its inmates after a period of re-purification, for, according to Bardic tradition exemplified by the Frisian Druids, "A state of eternal punishment is in itself impossible, and the infliction of such a punishment is the only act which the Deity cannot commit".

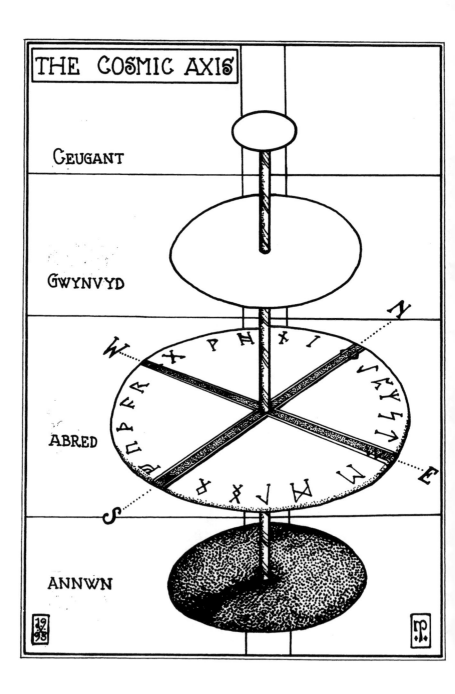

Chapter 4

The Pillar Above the Centre

The hazardous out-of-the-body journey of the trance magician, witch-doctor or shaman, who accesses other worlds (or other states of consciousness) by way of the cosmic axis, is recalled by the mythic journeys of Gods and heroes through the axis between the worlds. In Norse cosmology, the very name of the tree Yggdrassill has the meaning of 'The Horse of Ygg', Ygg being one of the many by-names used bardically to describe Odin. Here, there is a parallel between the cosmic axis and the artificial hobbyhorse used by dancers in customary festivities. The Celtic tale of *The Descent Into Annwn* and the Nordic legend of the journey downwards to visit Hel to reclaim the murdered god Balder are parallels of this shamanic experience. Likewise, in Druidic symbolism, the ascent of the soul into Gwynvyd uses the cosmic axis as its channel. Most notably, it is depicted in Hieronymus Bosch's painting *The Ascent into the Empyrean*, where souls are shown being led by angelic beings towards heaven through a tube of light. This vision and experience is one which those who have undergone near-death experiences will recognise. This vision is said by some to depict the Column of Glory of the Manichaean faith, which, according

---

Fig. 9. The Cosmic Axis, according to Druidic and Nordic principles. In the human being, this relates to the spinal column and the centres of energy within it.

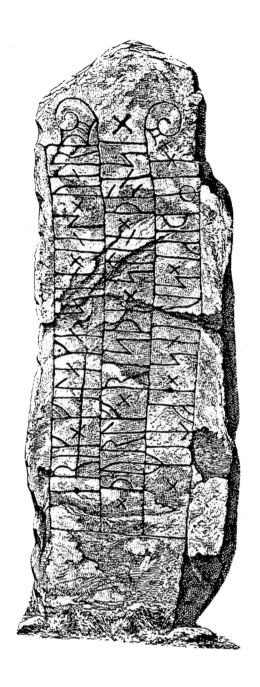

36

to this belief-system, is the channel through which prayers and souls enter the Heavenly Kingdom.

Undoubtedly, the cosmic axis is both a symbolic manner of explaining certain concepts of the realm of the sacred, and an actual description of the experiences of witches, shamans and those on the edge of death. These are genuine inner manifestations of the human constitution, reflected outwards into the world of symbol. Additionally, there is also the intriguing possibility that, in addition to its close resemblance to the Babylonian and Jewish palm-tree of life, the pictorial form of the Germanic Irminsul may have been derived from an infrequently-observed meteorological phenomenon. This is known technically as the Solar Halo Pillar, topped with a 'flared vee'. This phenomenon occurs occasionally in northern latitudes just at the moment of sunrise or set. As the magical protection of buildings, this shape was used on the gable-ends of 7th century Irish holy buildings, and in other sacred contexts, both Pagan and Christian.

The cosmological foundation of an important place by geomantic practitioners has an ideal symbolic form which reflects the cosmic axial pattern. In ancient Italy, where the tradition is first documented historically, the Etruscan Augurs used various mantic techniques to discover the correct geolocation for the centre of any new settlement. Once this was determined, it was marked by digging a pit or sinking a shaft into the ground beneath the future crossroads from which the rest of the area was to be laid out. This pit, known as the *mundus* was consecrated with offerings and then sealed with a

---

Fig. 10. A Danish commemorative runestone with typical inscription carved in three vertical rows, the centre of which represents the cosmic axis, with Irminsul-style scrolls at the top. The writing begins at the base of the central axis, continues in a sunwise direction down the right-hand side, then up again on the left to conclude at the top.

disc of stone that closely resembled a millstone. According to the Roman author Varro, this *mundus* was the gateway to the gods and goddesses of the Nether Regions. Once this pit had been dug, consecrated and sealed, and the stone or other upright marker had been erected over the shaft, then the official ceremonial foundation was deemed complete. To this day, a *mundus* exists in England at Royston in Hertfordshire, as a perfect cosmological pivot of the four quarters whose structure reproduces precisely the classical geomantic ordering of the landscape. Here is the crossroads of two of the four Royal Roads of Britain, Ermine Street and the Icknield Way. These sacred highways, of Roman or perhaps earlier provenance (according to Geoffrey of Monmouth the British king Belinus), were accorded the status of the King's Peace by several Saxon lawgivers including King Edward the Confessor. These roads were sacred ground, and the very name Roy Stone which is given to the megalith which stands even today by the crossways at the middle of the town, though it has been moved a little to permit the passage of motor vehicles, signifies a regal connection, bringing us back again to the connection between the centre point and the king.

Chapter 5

The Tree of Life

The tree is the most immediate natural symbol of the cosmic axis, for it is a living being that forms a link between the underworld of its roots through the middleworld surface of the soil onwards to the upperworld of the air. As a living being, each tree exists within a limited time-period, being born from an individual seed, growing through to maturity, reproducing, living to old age and then dying. Unlike a human being, however, whose body has a limited life, the tree can be sustained and regenerated almost indefinitely by means of cuttings, or, when cut down, by suckers arising from a still-living root system. Unlike their portrayals in botanical illustrations, real trees do not stand in isolation, for they provide shelter for many animals, and also support epiphytic and parasitic plants such as the mystic mistletoe. Furthermore, even when dead, trees are of great benefit to the human world, providing valuable material for the practitioners of craft, and fuel. As any woodcraftsperson knows, each species of wood possesses its own unique and precise characteristics, and ecologically, the different species of tree each occupy their own appropriate environmental niches, dependent upon specific conditions of soil, light and water.

Trees that stand singly in the open landscape, as opposed to those in groves, woods or forests, grow larger than those that must compete with their fellows, and so are prominent landmarks. Their special nature is recognised everywhere that materialist culture has not gained absolute ascendancy to

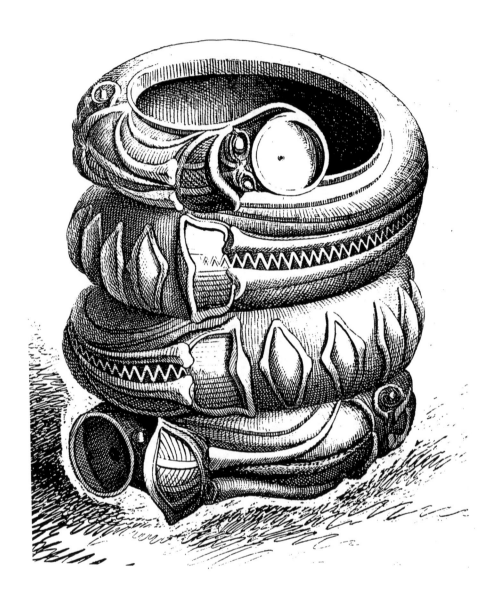

extinguish the final spark of spirit. These trees are infused with and stand as living representatives of the *anima loci*, the local spirit that empowers the place. Because of this, traditional society supports, protects and nurtures sacred single trees, and prevents their destruction. Folklore contains many stories concerning special sacred trees whose destruction has led to the downfall of their demolishers. The refusal of local inhabitants to comply with instructions to cut down fairy trees in Ireland are well known, even if only because they are quoted as examples of rustic credulity by materialists who wish to denigrate such things.

Whilst certain Christian holy men like St Martin of Tours assumed it to be their doctrinal duty to cut down the sacred trees of the Elder Faith, other, less destructive Christian holy men recognised the eternal symbolism of the tree of life inherent in every Pagan holy tree. Frequently Pagan sacred trees remained untouched when holy places were taken over by the Church. Many churchyard Yew trees pre-date the establishment of a church there, and in some cases have outlived the church, having survived to see the abandonment and demolition of the church, too. Such ancient holy trees remained at the fane when the Pagan sacred enclosure was appropriated by the incoming faith. But there are exceptions, for trees superseded by churches are less likely to have survived if those trees stood directly over the perceived centre of energy, as the ecclesiolatrists needed to erect their edifices directly over the site.

Trees planted in villages as markers and symbolic protectors of the community, however, many of which still survive, are likely

---

Fig. 11. The Celtic conception of the Nwyvre as manifested in multivalent metallic form in an Iron Age armlet from Scotland. When worn, the power of the Nwyvre is made visible, coiling along the arm of the wearer as an emblem of otherworldly communion.

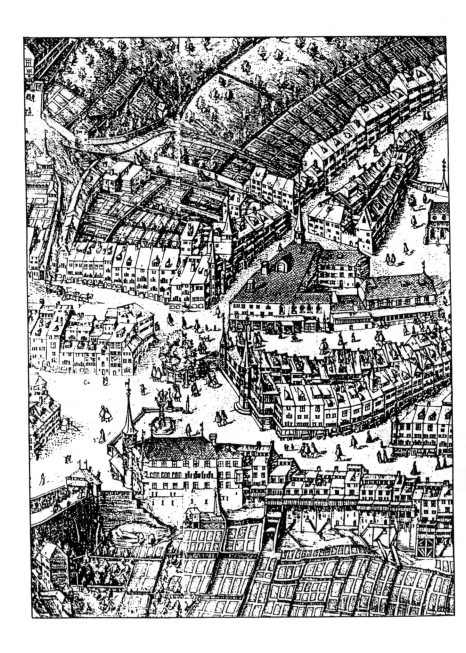

to stand at significant places. The sadly destroyed Merlin's Oak at Carmarthen, was one such tree, which even had its own local ditty, "When Merlin's Tree shall tumble down, Then shall fall Carmarthen town", which reflected the spiritual sustenance that the tree symbolised to the town. In the nineteenth century, it was killed deliberately by a chapel-going Protestant Christian who did not like it, or the neighbours who assembled there to pass the time of day. Subsequently, its remains stood, dead, by the roadside, until, not too long ago, it was hauled off to the museum. Similarly, the linden tree, planted in 1476 in the middle of the city of Fribourg in Switzerland, grew and flourished as a symbolic commemoration of the foundation of a new order.

Named the Murtenlinde, this venerable linden stood in a triangular enclosure in the middle of the road near to St George's Fountain and the City Hall. The overhead electric power lines for the city's trolleybus system were slewed from their straight alignment to clear it, but traffic was finally its downfall, for in 1983, on the unlucky date of the 13th of April, a drunken driver rammed his car into the linden, causing, as it turned out, fatal damage to the tree. In 1984, the one or two remaining branches still bore leaves, but in 1985, the venerable Lime was declared dead, and cut down. A new tree, genetically identical with the Murtenlinde, grown from a cutting, was planted, sadly not on the site of the old tree, but in the enclosure in front of the Town Hall near to the fountain of St George. Even that caused some motorists to complain, as some car parking spaces were abolished for the new tree. Despite the alteration of the tree-siting by a few metres, Fribourg's citizens

Fig. 12. A Swiss engraving from the year 1606 by Martin Martini, showing the centre of the city of Fribourg with the Murtenlinde and St George's fountain at the centre. The fountain remains, whilst the tree, planted in 1476, succumbed to traffic in the 1980s.

nevertheless maintained the tradition, a spirit sadly lacking in their Welsh counterparts in Carmarthen.

The Fribourg Murtenlinde was a notable example of the village or town lime tree, called in German *Dorflinde,* a number of which grow at various locations on the European mainland. The best of them have a form which reflects the layered arrangement of the cosmic axis, resembling Breugel's painting down to the supports which link the lowest tier to the ground. In the early part of the twentieth century, a considerable number of such trained lindens still grew, but the ravages of war, traffic and changes in fashion have meant that the majority of them are no more.

The common location for such geomantic trees is at road junctions in the often triangular area known as No Man's Land, after which the free-fire zone between the trenches in World War I was named. The remains of the great village Oak at Great Yeldham in Suffolk still shows the classic location of the village tree on its geomantically-appropriate site as local representative of the cosmic axis tree of life. When they are acknowledged, such central trees form the pivot of village or town life, serving as the centre-point for festivals and the collective celebration great events. In germany, they were the sites of local judgement, proclamations and festivities. As in Britain, wars put paid to the traditions. The last German village to hold local convocations under the linden tree was Unterwörnitz in Württemberg, where meetings were suspended in 1940, never to resume.

In England, the dressing of oaks and other trees with garlands, flags and bunting on Oak Apple Day, May 29th, ostensibly in commemoration of the escape of King Charles II from the forces of Parliament by hiding up an oak tree, was formerly a widespread custom in rural England. Dressing the Black Poplar tree growing at the crossroads at Aston-on-Clun in Shropshire is continued to this day. Generally the dressing of sacred trees and bushes with votive offerings of flags or cloths is closely related to the erection and decoration of Maypoles and other sacred representations of the Cosmic Axis, like the Pagan roofed poles of Lithuania. Decking certain fairy trees and bushes that stand, like Yggdrassil, as guardians of holy wells, can be seen in certain parts of Scotland, Ireland and Wales..

Trained Limes, Dorflinden and Royal Oaks are allied to the famous Cross Trees of Westphalia noted by the German antiquary Wilhelm Brockpähler who observed that such trees were once the sites of important judicial assemblies. Their form, trained to make a crossbar, distinguishes them from the three- or four-tiered Dorflinde. Their unique form appears to be related to the Druidical tradition described by Dudley Wright in the early part of this century in his esoteric book *Druidism: The Ancient Faith of Britain*: "The cross as a symbol, was known and revered by the ancient Druids, and their mode of consecrating an oak tree was first to fasten a cross beam upon it if the two main arms were not sufficiently prominent. Upon the right branch they cut in the bark, in fair characters, the word HESUS; upon the middle or upright stem, the word TARANIS; and on the left branch, the word BELENUS. Over all, and above the branching out of the arms, they inscribed the word THAU".

Chapter 6

Cross Trees and Maypoles

The customary geomantic traditions of Westphalia, which include the sixteen-foot-square Mystic Plot of the Vehmgericht are an important source of information on the customary practices of Pagan Europe. Brockpähler noted the distinction between the geolocation of Cross Trees and Dorflinden: Cross Trees are located either at the entrance to a community, or out in open country away from buildings, where they serve as landmarks or the sites of juridicial assembly. Dorflinden, on the other hand, are always situated at central *omphaloi,* the village's geomantic navel. The dances and fairs which took place around these trees involved various festivities, dressing the local tree and enacting plays or dances with deep symbolic content, often with significant characters from folk-tradition such as Jack-in-the Green and St George.

It is not a long jump from dancing round bedecked trees to erecting cut-down trees as maypoles. In Germany, as formerly in parts of Great Britain and Ireland, the Maypole is frequently a whole tree, felled on May Eve (Walpurgisnacht), upon which some or all branches are allowed to remain. Often an intact birch tree is decked with ribbons. In Wales, before the traditions were extirpated by evangelical Protestantism, the pole was a Birch tree, the *bedwen haf* (summer Birch) or *bedwen Fai* (May Birch).

In Northern Tradition spirituality, the Birch is a tree of purification and fertility. On a deeper level of anthropomorphic symbolism the Maypole represents the human phallus, which is only erect at times of intense sexual arousal, which, in terms of the year, is the Merry Month of May.

The pole tradition is very ancient. Certain Bronze-age Scandinavian rock-carvings appear to show sacral poles. A group of men carrying a tree is depicted on the Gundestrup Cauldron, the celebrated first-century CE Celto-Slavonic silver vessel found in Denmark. The 16th century English Protestant fundamentalist writer Stubbes disapprovingly noted the current importance of the Maying ceremonies. When the pole was 'brought home', it was drawn by a team of draught animals: "They have twenty or forty yoke of oxen, every ox having a sweet nosegay of flowers on the tip of his horns; and these oxen draw home this May-pole....which is covered over with flowers and herbs, bound round with strings from the top to the bottom, and sometimes painted with variable colours...".

In many parts of England, the leader of the Maying party is known as Robin Hood or Jack-in-the-Green. He personifies the incoming summertime. He is personated by a man covered in a frame decked with leaves and flowers. In this guise, he dances through the village with the May revellers. Often, Jack-in-the-Green is accompanied by his female consort, Maid Marian, who, traditionally is played by a man, but in more recent times, frequently by a woman. In addition to Maid Marian, Jack-in-the-Green was often accompanied by other guising people, such as Hobby Horses, sooty-faced chimney-sweeps, and masked figures. Although they have declined in Britain, mask-wearing customs continue to flourish in central Europe. In English Maypole dancing, each dancer holds a ribbon, During the dance, the dancers wind their way in and out of each other, gradually weaving ribbon patterns around the pole.

Current Maypole traditions in Germany range from freshly-cut whole trees, complete with leaves, to painted Maypoles. There is even a permanent Maypole with plastic garlands in the street in Speyer. In much of southern Germany, Maypoles are made

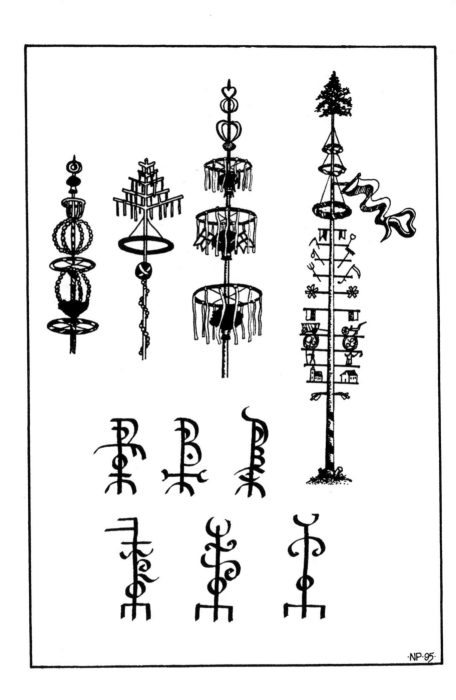

from conifers which retain a small amount of foliage at the top. In Bavaria, Maypoles are often painted with a spiral in blue and white, the Bavarian national colours. An English parallel, a permanent Maypole painted in red, white and blue, the British national colours, stands on the village green at Wellow in Nottinghamshire. A gilded weathercock adorns the summit of the Wellow pole.

Many Maypoles bear circular garlands which hang at various levels, representing the planes on the cosmic axis. Occasionally, there are side branches bearing the symbols of the trades and professions of the village, making the pole a definite representative of the whole community, symbolising the fundamental necessity of business to everyday life, and the authority of the local trades' guilds. Prudence Jones reports that sometimes Maypoles had a broomstick attached to the top in place of the uncut foliage, but I have never seen this in my Maytime travels either England or Germany. Much more rarely, Maypoles have been set up on steps, reproducing the cosmic axis - world mountain correspondence.

Unfortunately for folk-tradition, England today has still not recovered from the blow against Maytide festivities that came at the hands of Christian fundamentalists under Cromwell's Parliamentary republic in the mid-17th century. At that time, most of the dual faith celebrations, in which Pagan, Christian and other elements are intertwined in a festival which has its own character, such as Christmas and Martinmas, were suppressed by order of Parliament. In April 1644, the

---

Fig. 13. The cosmic axial form taken by Easter staves and Maypoles is reflected in the magical staves of the Northern Tradition. They are all representations of order in the image of the cosmic axis, which is manifested in humanoid form through anthropomorphic deities. Upper row of staves: 1. Freyr; 2. Fjölnir; 3. Fengur; Lower line: 1. Thundur; 2. Thekkur; 3. Thrumur.

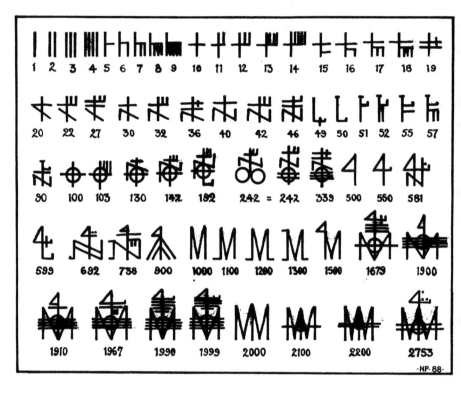

government ordered the eradication of all permanent Maypoles, and after the overthrow of the Commonwealth, many were never re-erected. A number of English villages, however, maintain the custom, and it is not impossible to restore the tradition elsewhere, if the will exists to do so.

The extirpation of the majority of permanent poles was of course a much easier proposition for fanatics than the abolition of tree-related custom. Local observance in private homes or on private, isolated, land, is almost impossible to police, and it is always in these quiet contexts that folk-practices continue. In 1912, for example, the folklorist E.M. Leather noted that it was then the practice in Herefordshire to fell a tall birch on May Day, to deck it with streamers and to set it against the stable door to bring good luck for that year. Similar customs continue in south Germany, though they are rare if not extinct in western England. The spiritual protection of the stables continued the horse-tree connection evident in the name Yggdrassill. Also, until the middle of the last century, it was a widespread custom for farmers in that part of the country to make crosses of birch and rowan twigs and to place them over doors on May morning. Like the birch, these would be left in place until the next May Day. Seed-beds and pigsties were protected likewise by these sacred woods on May Morn.

Another aspect of the cosmic axis and the sacred tree is the legend of a holy man or woman's stave that puts forth leaves when pushed into the ground at a geomantically-significant point. The staff then grows into a tree with which are associated miraculous healings or other wonders and portents.

Fig. 14. Stave-numbers are an alternative to using Arabic numerals to record dates. They are based upon the more ancient European system of notation, and make attractive ornamental sigils that can enhance artwork.

This staff-sprouting tale is told of the stave of Joseph of Arimathea at Glastonbury in Somerset, which became the Holy Thorn on Wearyall Hill, and of St Etheldreda at Etheldredestow in Lincolnshire, which became a great Ash-tree. The latter incident is recorded in a carved capital of a pillar in Ely Cathedral. By earthing the stave at such a point, it is revitalised, growing anew. In turn, it revitalises and empowers the surroundings with spiritual energy.

Chapter 7

The Symbolic Fairground

The Maypole and its festivities naturally encouraged the congregation of many people in the same place, and in many locations, May Fairs were an important part of the annual social cycle. The exclusive district of London's West End called Mayfair is a place-name reminder of this custom. Laid out according to the symbolic geomancy of the Holy City, medieval European fairs were conducted with symbolic ceremonies, many of them redolent of the lore of the cosmic axis.

For instance, at the Honiton Fair (formerly held on Whitmonday each year), the festivities, entertainment and trading were inaugurated by the Town Crier, who recited the formula: "Oyez, Oyez, Oyez, The glove is up and the fair has begun. No man shall be arrested until the glove is taken down. God save the King!". A pole bearing a glove, the emblem of regal authority, was erected, and the King's Peace reigned through the fair's duration. Old French playing cards often show certain kings, especially St Louis and Henri IV, holding sceptres on the end of which bears the anthropomorphic symbol of authorisation, the hand.

The hand also appears as a motif among the carvings in the Royston Cave, and as a wooden hand nailed to the wall in St Oswald's Church in Lower Peover in Cheshire. When the Northumbrian king Oswald, was slain a battle he fought against the Mercians led by the Pagan hero-king Penda, Oswald's dismembered head and arms were set up on posts.

Similarly, in the earlier Anglo-Saxon poem, Beowulf, the ripped-off arm of the monster Grendel is nailed to the gable-end of the hall, so the glove may be a bowdlerized relic of the erection of real human parts in more barbarous times.

The layout of fairs was deliberate and planned. At the centre was the pole, known in Norman French as *pau or pal* which bore the lordly emblem, such as glove or crest. The foundation of towns and fairs was enacted according to identical principles. In the middle ages, the erection of the pal marked the foundation of a new town in exactly the same way as the sealing of the *mundus* had to the Etruscan Discipline that the later Roman Augurs and medieval Locators used in modified form. Although most fairs gradually altered in character until they became little more than funfairs, complete with mechanised rides and side-shows, the tradition of their layout has remained until the present day. Fair people form a close-knit community which has to have the knowledge and ability to deal with the specialised problems inherent in their unique way of life. To have continuity, every specialised community preserves within itself a craft knowledge of how to accomplish the required tasks. This always includes traditions and rites which are often incomprehensible or just unrecognised by outsiders, who have no understanding of the necessities and principles involved.

An incident which occurred in England in 1943 demonstrates the continuity of just such a geomantic tradition among travelling showpeople. In December of that year, Pat Collins,

Fig. 15. The proclamation of a Nordic king, who by standing in the footprints on the sacred stone of kingship occupies the position of king both in the physical and the figurative senses, being empowered by the stable power of the earth as symbolised by the stone. When he is not present, his footprints mark the invisible body-space that stands above the stone's surface. Engraving from the works of Olaus Magnus.

IIII

EMPEROR

'The King of the Showmen' died. Although it was conduced in the depths of World War II, a period of dire austerity, Collins's funeral was a major event for the community of fair-people. It was reported in *The Sunday Express* on December 12, 1943 in an article titled "60-Year Ritual Fixed Grave for Showman 'King'" ". In it, the journalist wrote: "There was a strange incident at the cemetery when the old man's son visited it accompanied by Father Hanrahan, of St Peter's Catholic Church, Bloxwich, to select a site for the grave. When he came to seek a site for his father's last resting place it was found that the Catholic portion of the cemetery was full. The adjoining land which belongs to the cemetery was specially consecrated. When Mr Collins went to select a place for its first grave, he brought his foot forward, raised it and brought his heel down sharply on the turf, making a deep dent in it, exclaiming as he did so "This is the spot. I want the exact centre of my father's grave to be over that mark". He explained to the priest: "My father used those words and that gesture for 60 years every time that he inspected a fairground site to indicate where the principal attraction, usually the biggest of the merry-go-rounds, was to be erected. He never measured the ground, but the chosen spot was always in the exact centre of the showground. It was a ritual with him"."

There is a clear symbolic connection between the centre of the showground, the cosmic axis and the rotation of the merry-go-round. Furthermore, the burial of an important person at the *omphalos* of a new graveyard has great symbolic value. The body lies in the *mundus* in the earth at a point that links the

---

Fig. 16. The image of The Emperor, from the author's *Way of the Eight Winds Tarot*. In this card, I have used several symbols of authority: the *Reichsadler*, the Eagle symbol of the Holy Roman Empire; St George killing the dragon; the Sturgeon, an imperial fish; geometrical patterns, representing cosmic order; the orb of the world and the cosmic-axial sceptre; throne and Nwyvre beneath the Emperor's feet.

underworld with the world above. The fixation of the burial place by the same means as the geolocation of the centre of a fair shows that the geomantic principles of what are now considered to be separate, sacred and profane, are identical.

Making a footprint, symbolising in Celtic tradition ownership of the land, and by extension, kingship, is enshrined in the locator's traditional rite of bringing down the heel. Called in the parlance of Rugby Football 'making a mark', deliberately marking the ground with the foot is an example of authentic geomantic continuity from former times into the present. The footprint stones still extant in parts of Scotland and Ireland are almost all said to be places where clan chieftains, lords or even kings were proclaimed before their assembled followers. The further possibility that dancing around the Maypole or a labyrinth may have been superseded at some point by mechanical merry-go-rounds cannot be discounted. Unfortunately, the lack of historical documentation of fairs, discouraged since 'Puritan' times by governments and shunned by the ruling class, makes this difficult to verify.

What is certain is that traditional fairs associated with important gatherings, like the great Midsummer Fair of Cambridge, which has continued unbroken since it was founded by King John in 1208, were laid out as a microcosm of the country itself. As in the traditional town, where the different trades and occupations are located in their own characteristic districts, the stalls of various trades and crafts were allocated their own rows within the fair's grid-pattern. In certain instances, the disposition of the trades within the fair or town reflected their relative astrological characteristics. In a number

---

Fig. 17. Cross and perron-sigils can be used as a kind of personal heraldry, as here in German medieval and renaissance manuscripts, where they took the place of seals or signatures.

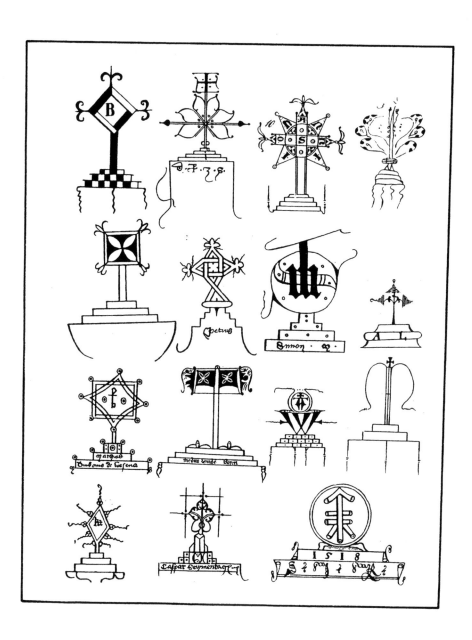

of instances, these temporary rows of stalls or booths gradually metamorphosed into permanent streets of buildings, and their successors stand still in these configurations. The town of St Ives in Cambridgeshire (formerly Huntingdonshire) has a grid-pattern derived from the ancient St Audrey's Fair of Slepe, which is held annually in the streets of the town in the week nearest October 17, St Etheldreda's Day.

Similarly, in the district of Barnwell in the city of Cambridge, the streets called Oyster Row, Mercers Row and Garlic Row are the permanent reminders both in their layout and names of the street grid of the once-mighty Sturbridge Fair, whose plan was unchanged for centuries. In such fairs, jurisdiction was under a special local law, the King's Peace, which lasted for the legal duration of the fair within the boundaries of the fairground. The presence of the King's Peace was represented in physical form by the pole, which at Sturbridge stood in the centre of the square called The Duddery, where 'duds' - clothes - were on sale. Law and order within the fair was dealt with by the Court of Pie Powder, from the French pied poudre, which means dusty feet. This was a court of summary jurisdiction, empowered to punish convicted offenders with an immediate spell in the stocks or on the pillory. Several such courts continued to sit at fairs in England until 1939, when World War II finally put an end to them. They included the fairs at Newcastle-upon-Tyne, Guildford, Ely and Bristol. The Court of Pie Powder at Sturbridge was convened each year until the fair's demise in 1932.

Chapter 8

The Witch's Broomstick

Elevation of the glove on a pole, signifying commencement of Pie Powder jurisdiction, that is, suspending the normal course of events, is paralleled in the custom observed in East Anglia, where a besom displayed with the twigs uppermost (as on the Maypoles) indicates that the lady of the house is away and the husband is free to dally with other women. Prudence Jones tells that in 1978 the Green Man pub at Gosfield displayed a broomstick above the inn sign only when the landlady was absent! Whatever secret activities of the phallus it denotes to those in the know, the symbolism of the witch's broomstick is closely related to the cosmic axis.

In East Anglian tradition, the staff of the broom is made of ash wood, sacred in modern Wicca to the World-Goddess, and in the Northern Tradition to Odin. The twigs which compose the besom proper are taken from the Birch, signifying purification; the Hazel, for initiation; and Rowan, for healing. There is a direct parallel here with the protective crosses used in Herefordshire on the other side of England. In East Anglia, the besom's twigs are bound to the ashen stave with withies taken from the Willow tree. In the Germanic branch of the Northern Tradition, the broom is associated with thunder. A certain type of magical broom called the *Donnerbeson* (Thunderbroom) is used to ward off lightning. This Thunderbroom symbol can be seen carved in wood, moulded in plaster or laid in brickwork patterns on many old buildings in Germany. There are also a few to be seen on Edwardian houses in Abbey Wood, south

London. In the Bardic tradition, the besom has a relation to the ancient Ogham alphabet, which is based on the twigs and branches of sacred trees. Here, it is called the *Dasgubell Rodd*, the *gift besom* which is used to sweep away all things that conceals the truth. The Druidic text called *The Book of Symbols* gives the following teaching concerning the Dasgubell Rodd:

Question: What is the Dasgubell Rodd?
Answer: The keys to the primitive Coelbren [the ancient Bardic alphabet - N.P.].
Q.   : What is it that explains the primitive Coelbren?
A.   : The Dasgubell Rodd.
Q.   : What else?
A.   : The secret of the Dasgubell Rodd.
Q.   : What secret?
A.   : The secret of the Bards of Britain.

According to British Druidic teaching, the besom or broomstick is the key to an encoded mystery which is open to interpretation either as a literal cryptographic key, or as the mystical, symbolic grasp of the entire mystery. The composition of the besom from various woods, constructed according to certain mystical dimensions, has a direct connection with Oghams and Runic staves, making the besom readable in a direct as well as a symbolic way.

The phallic or dildo-like nature of the witch's broomstick is well explored by wiccan writers, but equally it is symbolic of the cosmic axis along which the witch 'flies' in trance or out-of-the-body experiences. In addition to the stick, witches have been reputed to use alternative tools for flying. In the Maying

---

Fig. 18. The Witches' Meeting, to which they ride on pitchforks as an alternative to the broomstick. In performing rituals skyclad, we are, as microcosms, in direct contact with the macrocosm, where nothing comes between.

ceremonies of Sussex, it is customary for the female dancers to carry broomsticks, whilst the men carry pitchforks. At Hitchin in Hertfordshire, the Molly Dancer character called Mad Moll carried a wooden spoon and her husband carried the besom. Also, the pitchfork, hoe, rake and scythe, common agricultural implements, each have a symbolic meaning beyond the solely functional. They appear frequently on German maypoles.

Apart from the straws reputed to be ridden by Irish witches and the hurdle favoured in Essex and Cambridgeshire, the distaff was commonly ascribed a wiccan function. A famous medieval mural in Schleswig Cathedral in Germany shows the Goddess Frigg riding on a distaff in characteristic wiccan pose. This goddess, consort of Odin, possesses several attributes, one of which is the presentation of the flax plant to the human race, and the means of spinning linen from it. The goddess's major attribute is thus the distaff, and secondarily, the spindle, onto which the processed thread is spun. The connection between the spindle - the cosmic axis - and the distaff can be seen also in the ancient Saxon names for various celestial constellations now known more familiarly by their classical names. In Northern Tradition astronomy,he arrangement commonly called The Belt of Orion is known as Frigg's Distaff. The Pole Star, equivalent to the spindle, is in the Northern Tradition constellation called The Lady's Wain. Thus it could be argued that Frigg spans the visible heavens, the Pole Star held as the spindle in one hand, and with the distaff held between the knees. A full description of Northern Tradition astronomy and astrology can be found in the author's book *Runic Astrology* (Capall Bann 1995). The symbolic parallel between the Pagan goddess Frigg and the Christian demigoddess known as The Virgin Mary in her aspect as the Queen of Heaven is obvious. Both are portrayed as having a starry cloak, and Mary sits upon a crescent moon in traditional Catholic images.

Spinning has yet another connection with the cosmic axis and Royal Roads as sacred ground, for at the beginning of this century, the witchcraft researcher C.G. Leland reported that in his day, the witches of the Slavonian Romani met at crossroads to spin. In earlier days, ancient Italian law forbade women from spinning whilst walking along any road, as such actions were thought to stunt the growing crops. Spinning also carries the symbolism of the Fates, for the three Moirae of Greek mythology - Atropos, Lachesis and Clotho - span the fates of humans, and cut off the thread of life. Likewise, further north, the three Norns - Urd, Verdandi and Skuld - likewise spun, weaved and cut at the holy well at the base of Yggdrassill, determining the fate of human beings. The symbolism of the unwinding thread, the developing life, the clue to the labyrinth, are all encapsulated in the mysteries of the distaff and spindle. In English parlance, the distaff side of a family means the female, and this may have a greater significance than a mere allusion to the traditional tasks of woman.

Chapter 9

Spinning Space and Time

In Nordic religion, the heavens are ruled by the goddess Frigg, whose major attributes are the distaff and spindle. Because the sky appears to turn above the earth, with the North Pole as its axis-point. This is interpreted anthropomorphically as the human craft of spinning, in which the major function is the winding of thread around a turning spindle. Even the word *wyrd* which bears the connotations of destiny and becoming is connected with the Old High German words *wirt* and *wirtel*, meaning 'spindle'. Thus, spinning thread on a spindle and the allied craft of weaving on a loom are connected allegorically or magically with time and destiny.

Spinning is an act of creation in which the disordered, and unusable, fibres of wool or flax are transformed by human skill into a ordered, and usable, thread. Order is brought out of chaos by re-aligning its materials by employing energy, time

---

Fig. 19. Because the eightfold is a symbol of order and completion, the *Aegishjalmur* or Eagershelm is considered the greatest image of magical power in the north. Taken from the brow of the dragon Fafner when Siegfried killed it, this 'helm of awe' brings irresistable power to its wearer. Top left: the Eagershelm; top right: the eightfold Star of Heaven; below left: as a powerful magical sigil in the European martial arts, it is shown as the helm-crest of the Sussex knight Sir John de Warenne, from 1329; below right: medieval eight-mark perron from Gilling West, Durham.

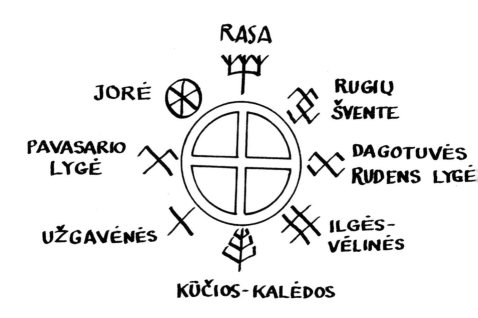

RASA

JORĖ

RUGIŲ
ŠVENTE

PAVASARIO
LYGĖ

DAGOTUVĖS
RUDENS LYGĖ

UŽGAVĖNĖS

ILGĖS-
VĖLINĖS

KŪČIOS-KALĖDOS

and the power of the conscious will. There are two tools necessary for spinning - the spindle and the distaff. The spindle is rotated to spin the thread and the spun material is gathered onto the distaff.

In northern Europe, the turning spindle, like the water-mill, is a prime symbolic model of the cosmos. It works according to a rhythmic, reciprocating, cyclic, motion from which flows an unbroken stream of thread that symbolises the continuum of undying existence. The spindle of the heavens, around which the fixed stars appear to rotate, is marked by the Pole Star. This star, which stands directly above the North Pole, has been given several poetic names, including The Guiding Star, The Lode Star, God's Nail and The Nowl. It is the 'leading star' of the navigators of old, upon which traditional East Anglian gardeners still orientate their rows of seeds at planting time. Each year, at Yuletide, it is recalled by the artificial star placed on top of the Christmas Tree.

Cosmologically, this 'loom of creation' is related directly to the apparent motion of the sun through each day and also through the year. This is one of the many symbolic meanings of the labyrinth, more specifically the ball of thread, which, in many labyrinth-myths, enables the hero to find his way through its twists and turns. In the symbolism of weaving, the sun creates the fabric of time on the loom of the Earth. The warp, the threads that run in a north to south direction, is laid down by the Earth Mother, and the sun goddess completes the fabric by weaving the east-west threads. It is the intervention of human

---

Fig. 20. The eight festivals of the year, in the contemporary Lithuanian and Latvian Pagan tradition, with corresponding sigils. The British Pagan parallels are: Rasa, Midsummer solstice; Rugiu - Svente, Lammas; Dagotuves - Rudens Lyge, autumnal equinox; Ilges -Vélines, Samhain; Kucios-Kaledos, midwinter; Uzgavenes, Imbolc; Pavasario - Lyge, vernal equinox; Jore, St George's Day/ May Day.

beings as the third element that creates the fabric-patterns known as "the Web of Wyrd" and "the rich tapestry of life".

Traditionally, the spindle-distaff symbol of the heavens, and the origin of Wyrd through its actions, is largely the preserve of the female principle. The weaving technique can be compared with the other great image of the cosmos, the water-mill. Like the turning of the heavens, the continued operation of the mill ensures the continuance of the human race by providing the staple diet, flour. Symbolically, the mill is a microcosmic image of the cosmos as traditionally conceived.

Although the familiar European windmill was invented in France around the year 1100, the vertical watermill is far older. The working parts of the traditional mill consisted of a channel beneath the floor of the mill, through which water was conducted. The flowing water in the channel drove the mill-paddles that were connected directly to an axletree. This rotating vertical axis carried the power upwards through the centre of the immobile lower millstone to the upper millstone, to which it was connected directly. Then, the upper millstone rotated above the fixed lower one.

Symbolically, the vertical watermill reflects the cosmic axis, the Earth and the Heavens. The immobile, fixed Earth was symbolised by the lower millstone. The cosmic axis - the axletree - passed through the millstone's centre, symbolising the *omphalos,* the navel of the human being or the world. The axis thus linked the lower, serpentine, flowing, watery underworld with the upper, starry, heavenly, upperworld, represented by the rotating upper millstone. Below *Calas* flowed *Nwyvre.* In the underworld, the dragon-like power of flowing water had a dual nature. Although it provided power to the millstone, it also threatened to gnaw away with rot the wooden paddles and axletree, like the serpent Nidhoggr gnaws at the roots of Yggdrassil.

70

This rotation of the four parts of the day or the four seasons of the year around the cosmic axis is portrayed in the 'four footed cross' known as the fylfot or swastika. In former times, this dynamic figure was seen as signifying movement and energy as an aspect of right orderliness. Thus, in the Northern Tradition, it is the Hammer of Thor, powerful maintainer of order against the dissolution wrought against the gods by ill-doing giants and trolls. Because this sign can be drawn in a left- or right-handed form, it was considered either male or female, outgoing or incoming, depending on the direction of 'turn'. Which is which has always been the subject of discussion, depending on whether the arms of the figure are taken to represent the leading edge of a hammer, or the trailing wisps of flame on a rotating fiery cross.

The history of this figure in the twentieth century is well known. From being a revered mystic sigil of spirituality, it was transformed in a few years into the emblem of militant anti-Semitism. Even this rapidly acquired its own mythology.

The fable that Adolf Hitler deliberately reversed a 'good' form of the swastika to make it 'evil' originated in a World War II British propaganda piece written by the science-fiction author, H.G. Wells, who was not known for his esoteric knowledge. Now this version of 'mythstory' is believed by millions.

Even a summary perusal of either ancient European or contemporary Oriental examples of the sign will show beyond doubt that both forms were and are used in pre- and non-Nazi times. But the truth never threatens a good 'urban belief tale', and, untrue though it is, this story has become part of the baggage that it must carry.

Contemporary folklore aside, the important aspect of the appropriation of the fylfot by Adolf Hitler is that it is the prime recent example of the wholesale taking-over of a sigil, and the transformation of its meaning into something quite different. Because, in the west, it has become literally the symbol of

National Socialism, it can be used no longer in its earlier context. Even half a century after the destruction of German fascism, the sigil is irrevocably associated with the Nazi regime. So it is impossible to use the swastika even to-day in an esoteric context without evoking visions of Auschwitz. The transformation of this sigil demonstrates that it is possible to transform the meaning of anything by means of a powerful on-lay, just as the Christians did with the cross. To-day, the fylfot's örlog is overburdened with the dark shadows of its use between 1919 and 1945. Whether the sigil will ever again be used in its spiritual context in the west is a matter of doubt.

As symbolised by the swastika or the cross-within-a-circle, the solar day has four parts. At sunrise, the sun climbs into the heavens to a culmination-point that is Midday, when the sun is in the south. This is the sun's first quarter. The second quarter of the sun sees its lowering in the sky as it moves westwards, finally setting. Then, invisibly, the sun enters its third quarter, when it continues lower until Midnight, when it is in the due north. The fourth quarter is between Midnight and sunrise, when the sun is below the horizon but coming up. This fourfold division is ever-changing. Only at the two equinoxes is it an equal fourfold division. During the winter half of the year, the dark 'quarters' are larger and longer than the light ones, whilst in the summer half, the light 'quarters' are longer and larger than the dark ones. Thus the quartering of the day is a dynamic one, ever in flux and never static. Similarly, the Moon shows its four quarters, in a monthly cycle.

Related to the quarters of the day are the Tides of the Day. As with all natural ways of perceiving the passing of time, these Tides are determined by the apparent motion of the sun as

Fig. 21. Emblematical wheel of the eight Tides of the Day, with corresponding 24-hour clock, compass directions of the sun at those hours, and circle of the runes of the Elder Futhark.

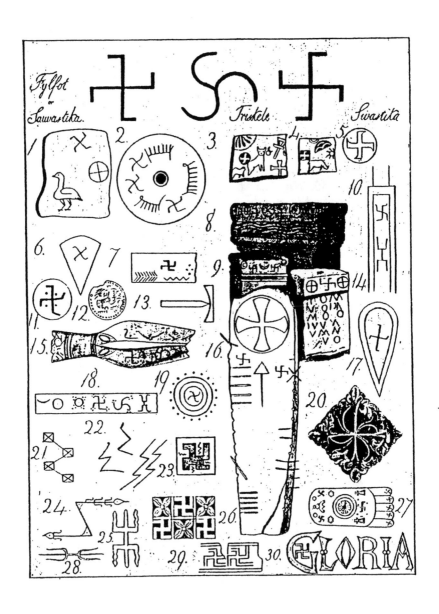

viewed from any place. They are not theoretical, like the Mean Time and Time Zones currently used by almost everybody. At any moment of day or night, the sun is actually in a definite direction from us. In daytime, we can actually see the sun in cloudless weather conditions, whilst at night, although the sun is 'beneath the earth', and consequently invisible to us, nevertheless it is also in a precise position with regard to us. This is the principle that underlies the construction of sundials.

Traditionally, the four quarters of space are related to the four seasons and identified by specific qualities that in turn are symbolised by colours. These colours vary completely from culture to culture, so there is no question that they are archetypal in some way. However, within the cultural conventions where they exist, they do have meaning. Hermetic colours, such as those used for the geomancy box sometimes employed in divination, have the orientated sides painted

Fig. 22. Ancient Swastikas and Thunderbolts, from H. Colley March's *The Fylfot and the Futhorc* Tyr (March's interpretations). 1. Archaic Greek pottery, 650 BCE, fylfot and aerial emblems; Terra-cotta balls, Troy, fylfot and flaming altar; 3,4: Indo-Scythian coins, 250 BCE, fylfot and rayed sun; 5: Stamped clay, Lake of Bourget, Switzerland; 6. Swastika as a maternal symbol on a lead goddess image from Troy; 7 Bracteate, Denmark, fylfot, meander and fire symbol; 8: Roman altar at High Rochester, dedicated to the goddess Minerva by Lucius Caecilius Optatus; 9: Roman altar from High Rochester, dedicated by Titus Licinus Valerianus to the standards of the faithful of the Varduli; 10: On bone arrow, Deanish bog; 11: Archaic Greek pottery, Santorini; 12: Norwegian bracteate; 13: Hammer of Thor; 14: Roman altar at Birdoswald; 15: Bronze spear-head from Brandenburg; 16: Irish Ogham stone, Aglish, co. Kerry; 17: Norman shield from the Bayeux Tapestry; 18: Scandinavian bracteate; 19: Annam stone; 20: Consecration cross, Salisbury Cathedral, 1220; 21: Chinese thunder scroll; 22: Lightning symbols; 23: Archaic Greek pottery, Rhodes; 24: Scandinavian thunderbolt, Forfarshire, Scotland; 25: Thunderbolt of Jupiter; 26: Border of a Christian clergyman's vestment, 1320; 27: Footprint of the Buddha; 28: Conventional thunderbolt; 29: Norwegian br; 30: Legend on church bell, Heathersage, 1617.

76

citrine, red, black and olive green, whilst some Islamic traditions use red, blue, green and yellow to denote the quarters.

Many contemporary practitioners of Northern Tradition spirituality follow a scheme which appears to be Celtic in origin. In this system, the north is black; the east red; the south white and the west, brown. These colours relate to the nature of time. The black northern quarter symbolises the darkness of night and the winter quarter of the year. Red in the east symbolises the 'morning-red', sunrising quarter of morning, or spring; whilst the white south denotes the brightness of the light of midday and summertime. Finally, the western quarter, brown in colour, symbolises the declining light of evening and the dying leaves of autumn.

Amid his fantastic De Selbyan theories of existence, in *The Third Policeman*, the Irish comic-fantasy writer Flann O'Brien accurately recalls the Celtic colour of the quarters, here described poetically as winds. According to O'Brien, the north wind is a hard black; the east is deep purple in colour; the south is a fine shining silver; whilst the west wind is amber. These are 'The Four Winds of Eirinn', which determine the birth-destiny of individuals. According to this Irish tradition, one's character and future life is determined by the wind that is blowing at the moment of one's birth.

The influential *Ten Books on Architecture* by the Roman master architect Vitruvius preserve for us the traditions of Roman location. These principles, detailed in Chapter 6 of Book I, take

---

Fig. 23. The appropriation of the swastika by the German National Socialists is exemplified in this advertisment for the *Deutscher Heimatkalender*, the official Nazi party calendar for 1937 (from the Ahnenerbe journal *Germanien,* 1936). As a solar symbol, the swastika on the banner carried by a brownshirt, reflects the rising sun as guardian of industry and agriculture, home and family.

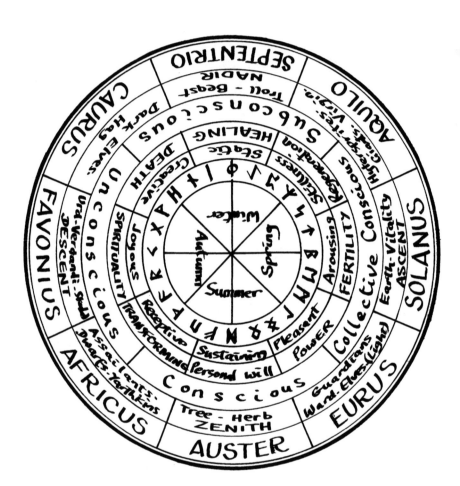

78

the winds into account in building. "Some have asserted that there are only four winds", writes Vitruvius, "Solanus from the due east; Auster from the south;, Favonius from due west; and Septentrio from the north. But the more careful investigators inform us that there are eight. The greatest of them was Andronicus of Cyrrhus, who, to demonstrate the principle, built the octagonal marble tower in Athens [The Tower of the Winds - N.P.]. He made carvings representing the winds, on each side of the octagon, facing the direction from which the wind blows; and on top, he placed a conical marble block upon which was a Triton with a rod outstretched in its right hand..."

To this day, the eight winds are known by their Latin names. In the northern eighth is the wind called Septentrio; to the north-eastern eighth is Aquilo; in the east, Solanus. Next, in the south-eastern airt, is Eurus, followed in the south by Auster. The south-western airt is covered by Africus, whilst the western is Favonius. Finally, in the north-west, is Caurus. Each wind represents a quality that the architect or magician might wish to use or exclude from his or her workings. These qualities also have a bearing on time, for each of the eight winds is identified with one of the eight Tides of the Day.

Concurrent with the eightfold division of the circle of the horizon into its eight airts, is the corresponding eightfold division of the daily solar cycle. In the Northern Tradition these eight airts mark the Eight Tides of the day, which overlap the four quarters. Four of the eight are wholly in a corresponding quarter, and four are each at the junction of two quarters. Of course, these Tides of the Day have no connection with the tidal ebb and flow of the sea, which obey a different cycle controlled

Fig. 24. The wheel of the eight winds, according to the teachings of *The Way of the Eight Winds*, showing correspondences of the winds to times of year, spiritual beings, human states of consciousness and qualities of existence.

by the interaction of the Moon, the Earth and the Sun. But, "Time and Tide wait for no man". Because the 24 hour day is divided by eight, each of the Tides of the Day lasts three hours. The cardinal or intercardinal direction, known as the ætting, lies at the exact middle of each Tide. Noon, for example, falls at the middle of Noontide or High Day, in the direction of due south. It is the time of day when the sun is at its highest point in the sky. Diametrically opposite this is Midnight, 12 p.m., which stands at the centre of the Tide of Midnight, with a direction of due north. This is at the middle-point of the night, when the sun, though unseen, is due north of the observer,

Esoterically, these eight airts are special times, for people born at these Tidal centre-points, known in East Anglia as the Chime Hours, have always been considered to have special psychic abilities. In the 24-hour clock, these Chime Hours are 3 AM, 6 AM, 9 AM, 12 Noon, 3 PM (15.00), 6 PM (18.00), 9 PM (21.00), and 12 Midnight (24.00) hours. In the English tradition, the first Tide of the day is between 4.30 AM and 7.30 AM. It is called Morntide, and has the esoteric quality of awakening, bringing liveliness and fertility. The second Tide, Daytide (otherwise Dæg Mæl, Undertid or Oander) runs between 7.30 and 10.30. Its esoteric quality is associated with work, particularised as earning money or physical gain. Next, the third Tide, Mid Day, runs between 10.30 and 13.30. It denotes the exercise of the personal will, sustenance and continuance. The fourth Tide runs from 13.30 until 16.30. It is called Undorne, or alternatively Ofanverthr Dagr or Oern. Its time-quality is that of receptiveness and transformation, which may be expressed in the function of being a parent of a child. Fifth is Eventide, from 16.30 to 19.30. Also called Midaften, it is the time of joyousness and spirituality, when one may enjoy family life. Next comes Night-Tide, from 19.30 until 22.30. Otherwise known as Ondverth Nott or Cwyl-tid, the sixth Tide of the Day is a time of creativity, teaching and learning. Between 22.30 and 1.30 AM is the Tide of Midnight, a static period of regeneration and healing. Finally, the eighth Tide of the Day is Uht, otherwise Ofanverth Nott or Uhten-tid, which occupies the day-cycle between 1.30 and 4.30 AM. This is a time of stillness, sleep, and even death.

The other branch of the Northern Tradition, the Celtic, divides the day into eight tides of three hours apiece. Like their Saxon and Norse counterparts, these tides are at their greatest power at their middle.

Thus in the Welsh tradition, Nawn (midday) and Dewaint (midnight) fall at the middle of their tides. The Welsh version of the eight tides is Dewaint (Midnight), which runs from 10.30 PM until 1.30 AM; Pylgeint (Dawning), from 1.30 AM until 4.30; Bore (Morningtide), from 4.30 until 7.30; and Anterth (The Tide of Vapourlessness), from 7.30 till 10.30. The tide of Nawn (Noontide) runs from 10.30 AM until 1.30 PM. Nawn is followed by Echwydd (Rest), from 1.30 until 4.30 PM. Next comes Gwechwydd (Eventide or Twilight), whose period extends from 4.30 until 7.30. The final tide is Ucher (Overcast or Disappearance), which runs from 7.30 until 10.30, when it is followed by Dewaint.

In addition to the Tides themselves are several important horizon-marks, some of which designate the beginning and end of Tides, and others which are in the middle of Tides:

Time	Modern English Name	Anglo-Saxon Name	Azimuth	Compass
00.00	Midnight (Low Noon)		0°	Due N.
04.30	Rising	Rismæl	67° 30'	ENE
07.30	Daymark	Dæg Mæl	112° 30'	ESE
12.00	Noon (High Noon)	Mid Dæg	180°	Due S.
16.30	Eykt	Eykt	247° 30'	WSW
19.30	Suppertime		292° 30'	WNW

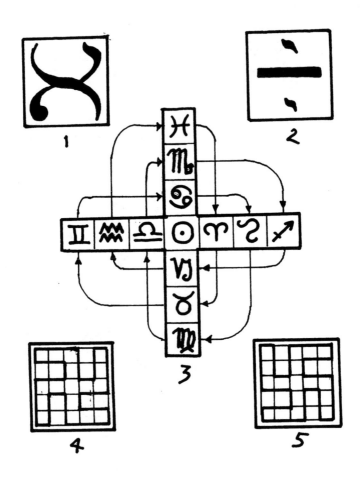

Chapter 10

Dancing With the Hobby Horse

An aspect of the broomstick not yet mentioned, related to its traditional use in witchcraft, is in the broom dance, where the dancer executes certain figures with a broom to music. This East Anglian tradition survives in a few places, but may well have been more widespread formerly. Little Downham was one such place. The broom dance of Comberton in Cambridgeshire, was rescued from extinction only a few years ago by Cyril Papworth, grandson of the village dancer, Tulla Papworth, with whom the dance was thought to have died. Cyril Papworth once wrote that it took him 36 years to learn to perform the dance properly. Among others, this complex broom dance has figures called "Fool's Jig" and "Hobby Horse". In addition to the broom dance, there are a number of local traditions where sacred processions are led by a pair of whifflers with brooms to sweep away from the road the evil spirits that cause bad luck, allowing the party of musicians and dancers to proceed without hindrance.

Closely related to the witch's broomstick and the cosmic tree is the hobby horse, a curious artifact which is generally seen hobnobbing with Molly Dancers or Morris Dancers and other traditional ceremonial performers at festivals of indigenous

Fig. 25. The Qabalistic Mystery of Aleph, according to Major-General J.F.C. Fuller: 1. The Hebrew letter aleph; 2. The beginning of motion through opposition, in the deconstruction of aleph into two yodin and a cross-bar which is vau; 3. The whirling forces of the zodiac; 4. The female swastika; 5. The male swastika. The 17 squares of the swastika refer to the mystic word IAO, whose esoteric numerical value is 17.

European folk-tradition. Hobby horses are a continuation of extremely ancient tradition, the earliest known representation of which is of a man in a horsehead mask, dating from the stone age and found in the Pinhole Cave in Derbyshire. Various forms of the hobby horse continue in use today both in Great Britain and mainland Europe. Perhaps the most celebrated is the hobby horse that is paraded through the Cornish town of Padstow on May Day each year. In the Padstow festival, May is welcomed at dusk on the previous calendar day, the ancient way of reckoning days, with the Padstow Night Song. In the morning, the Old Hoss is carried out from the Red Lion Inn, and paraded through town all day. The visible part of the horse is black and boat-shaped, and the horse part has a ferocious mask with snapping jaws.

Snapping is a characteristic of the Hobby Horse and similar guising beasts in other places. For instance, the Hooden Horse of Kent, which is paraded at Canterbury on Christmas Eve and other times, and Snap the Dragon, formerly paraded through Norwich. The attendant Whifflers who cleared the way for the Norwich dragon procession on St George's Day (April 23) carried ribbon-bedecked staves, whose form is allied to both hobby horses and broomsticks. The Padstow perambulation itself is attended by a man dressed in women's clothing, the Teaser. He directs the horse with a phallic padded club.

Now and again, the creature sinks to the ground as if dead, only to leap up again into life at a certain line in the Day Song which the accompanying musicians and singers performs

---

Fig. 26. The megalithic arch of the Oghams, according to Druidic teachings. Here, the letters of the alphabet are related to the supports and lintels of an entrance, which is the space of a human body. Thus, the letters of the alphabet, which are, in human terms, the image of existence, is related to the world of the physical human being.

continuously throughout the day. The horse chases after women and envelopes them under its skirts, which is said to bring them good luck - or a baby.

The horse festival at Padstow was associated traditionally with a Maypole, which was temporarily suspended in the 1870s and reinstated more recently. The pole itself was never a cut tree, but always a spar taken from the boatyard, which was set up at the top of Cross Street in the centre of a cross inlaid in stone, which was a prominent geomantic feature of the street. The pole was thus the cosmic axis, set at the navel of the town. Part of the earlier festivities involved carrying the horse through the streets to Traitor's Pool, a quarter of a mile out of town. Here, the horse pretended to drink. At Minehead, Somerset, another Hobby Horse, the Sailors' Horse, was taken to a crossroads early on May Morning, where it would bow to the rising sun. There is a legend associated with Padstow that St George visited the town, where his horse 'made a mark' with one of its hooves and brought forth a spring - St George's Well. This may have some connection with the Traitor's Pool visit, for the Padstow Day Song has an explicit reference to St George:

"Awake, St George, our English knight, O!
For summer is a-come, and winter is a-go,
And every day God give us his grace,
By day and by night, O!
Where is St George, where is he, O?
He is out in his long boat, all on the salt sea, O!
And in every land O! The land that ere we go."

The traditions of the broomstick and hobby-horse dancers in western Europe may be compared with those of the Buryat shamans of Baikal, whose rites and traditions preserve or at least appear to reflect some of the practices and lore of pre-civilised times throughout Central Asia and Europe, use ceremonial horse-staves made of wood or iron. They measure about 75 cm long, and are constructed with a horse's head and hooves at the ends. These staves symbolise the supernatural horse on which the shaman rides to the upper and lower worlds. In its power of trance-induction, these horse-staves are considered to be at one with the ritual drum, whose skin is naturally made of horse-hide. It is interesting that the traditional usages of Buriat shamanry appear to concur closely with the ancient usages of the broom dance and the hobby horse as aspects of the cosmic axis in Europe, whose music, drumming and dancing we witness today in the British May ceremonies.

.

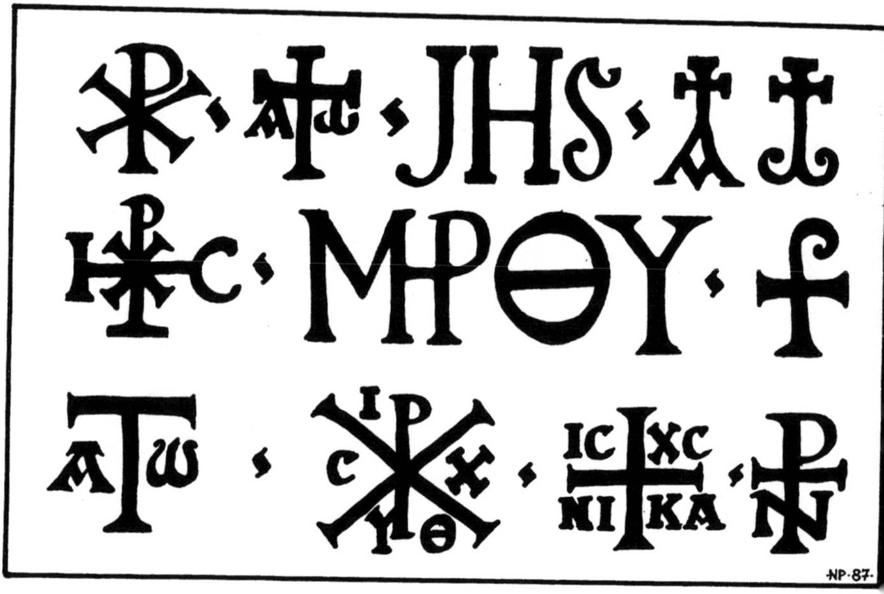
JHS
MPΘY
IC XC
NI KA
NP·87

Chapter 11

Alphabets, Sacred Monograms and the Cross

Many complex human concepts need to be expressed rapidly and concisely, and so fragments or abbreviations often serve to represent the whole of something. Archaic pictorial representations gradually were refined into stylised hieroglyphics, which in turn led to the invention of the alphabet. In turn, individual letters of the alphabet were used to describe certain aspects of existence, and in systems like Hebrew, Greek, Runic and Gothic, the system of correspondences is carried to a high art of symbolism. Combinations of letters such as bind-runes or monograms express a particular combination of letters' meanings.

Fig. 27. Monograms of the Names of God, from Roman Catholic and Greek Orthodox tradition. Top row: 1. Chi-Rho, monogram of the Christ; 2. Cross with *alpha* and *omega,* representing the two forms of wealth, *alpha* (cattle), movable, disposable wealth, and *omega* (land, homestead), immovable, non-negotiable wealth; JHS monogram representing *Jesus Hominem Salvator* (Jesus, saviour of men); 4. Variant forms of *alpha* and *omega.* Second row: 1. Chrismon, *Jesus Soter* (Jesus Saviour) and Jesus Christ combined; 2. Mother of God; 3. Alternative Chi-Rho in the form of labyrinth centre-pattern. Lowest row: 1. Tau cross with *alpha* and *omega;* 2. Chrismon with ichthys (fish), symbol of Jesus the fisherman; 3. Chrismon from the communion wafer used in the Greek Orthodox church, meaning Jesus Christ - Conquer; 4. Shorthand version of the preceding sigil.

Derived from the Byzantine fashion of signing documents with monograms made of the letters of the person's name, there are several Christian monograms that refer to the name of their son-god Jesus, or his title, 'Christ'. Monograms of 'Jesus' are restricted to the formula IHC, a Latinisation of some of the letters of the Greek name of Jesus, IHΣOYΣ. These Christian monograms are outside the mainstream of sacred sigils, either in the Jewish tradition, with which they are most closely connected, or the late antique Pagan manner. They are rather abbreviations or shorthand. IHC is rather a strange kind of abbreviation, like the name used centuries later by the German National Socialists for their secret police force, the Gestapo. Gestapo is a word made by the contraction of the unwieldy *Geheimstaatspolizei,* 'Secret State Police'. Such terminology was rightly condemned by George Orwell as 'Newspeak', but now it is, unfortunately, an integral part of British government regulatory bodies, like Ofwat, Oftel and Ofgas.

The earliest monogram for the Christ appears to have been the Chi-Rho sigil. This is a combination of the Greek letter for 'CH' and 'R', X and P. These are the first letters of the name XPIΣTOΣ, Christ. In its form, it sometimes appears as an open hooked letter Rho that resembles a shepherd's crook. Other versions of this do not have an X-shaped cross intersecting the upright, but a single arm. When this is open-ended it resembles closely the form we use to begin drawing a labyrinth, and it may have some historic connection with the labyrinth form, whose lore certainly has a strong Christian element. It can also be taken as symbolising the cosmic axis, intersected at its earthly *omphalos* by the crossroads.

Fig. 28. Symbolism of the church plan, based on the cross of Jesus, according to thirteenth century western masonic esotericism. The human body on the cross is a version of Vitruvian Man, where the human body is depicted within a geometrical framework similar to that in Thibault's diagram (fig. 3).

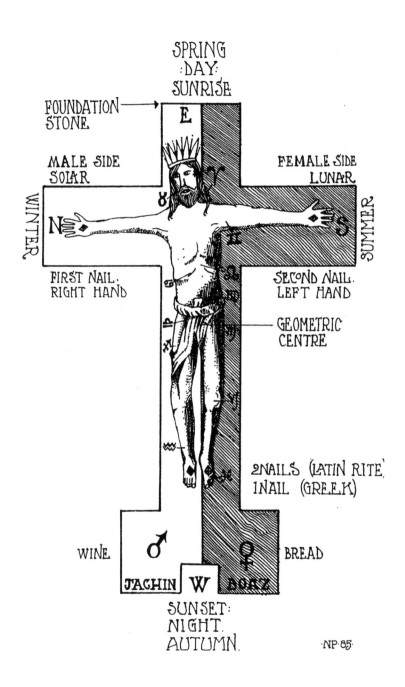

SPRING
·DAY·
SUNRISE

FOUNDATION STONE.

E

MALE SIDE SOLAR

FEMALE SIDE LUNAR

WINTER

N

S

SUMMER

FIRST NAIL.
RIGHT HAND

SECOND NAIL.
LEFT HAND

GEOMETRIC
CENTRE

2 NAILS (LATIN RITE)
1 NAIL (GREEK)

WINE

BREAD

JACHIN

W

BOAZ

SUNSET:
NIGHT.
AUTUMN.

·NP·85·

Although the monogram appears to have pre-dated the cross by several centuries as a Christian sign, it is the cross which is most associated with the religion. However, the cross as a sacred sign was neither invented by Christians nor did it signify at first the scaffold on which the founder of the religion was said to have been executed. Extant effigies of Assyrian kings, for example, show them wearing crosses around their necks. These are identical to those worn by medieval priests of the Celtic and Roman Catholic churches.

Dating from 800 years BCE, however, these Assyrian crosses have nothing to do with the Christian interpretation of existence. Later, the cross was used in the Roman Empire as a religious emblem by various pre- and para-Christian faiths. For example, an image of the lioness-headed goddess Sekhmet, discovered in the ruins of the Celto-Roman Temple of Mithras at Caernarfon in Wales, held an iron cross in her hand. It was of the form later assumed to be an exclusively Christian emblem. In Egypt around the same time, the Coptic Christian monk later canonised as saint Anthony used the Tau cross as his emblem. The Franciscans use it to-day.

From feudal times, the cross became an important element in heraldry, through a convergence of the Pagan emblems and sigils used in the various Northern Tradition warrior cults and the Christian symbolic cults of saints, each of whom had their own emblematical iconography. In the Crusades, it was adopted as the basic symbol of all knights and soldiers who fought Islam, and Popes allocated certain colours as identifying marks of individual units or nations. Thus, the flag of England became a red cross on a white field, Sweden a gold cross on blue, Denmark a white cross on a red field, and so on. The colours were not arbitrary, for they reflected symbolically the esoteric nature of the corresponding patron saints of the nation. Thus, the English flag is still known as the Cross of St George.

There were some exceptions to the crusaders' flags, though these also reflected the saintly attributes. The flag of the Scots, for instance, is a saltire, that is a white X on a dark blue ground, is the Cross of St Andrew, who, according to myth, was crucified on an X-shaped cross. St Patrick's Cross, which before the days of the Irish Republic was the flag of Ireland. It has a red saltire on a white background.

To-day, people professing to be followers of Satanism sometimes wear a Latin cross upside down. This, both they, and their self-proclaimed opponents, evangelical protestant fundamentalists, claim is an emblem of the Christian Devil. However, the 'inverted cross' is actually a standard sigil from Catholic Christianity, about which neither weekend evangelical Christians nor weekend Satanists seem to know much. Catholic mythology tells that when St Peter came to be killed for preaching the Christian religion. his tormentors wanted to crucify him in the manner of Jesus. But Peter insisted that he was not worthy of emulating his master in this way, and so, acquiescing to his request, the legal authorities inserted the cross in the ground with the head down. Thus, the inverted cross is not in any way a symbol of Satanism, but of Peter, the Rock upon which the Roman Catholic Church is founded. Unfortunately, such laughable confusion is symptomatic of the general unawareness of symbolic meaning that characterises even spiritual organisations in contemporary times.

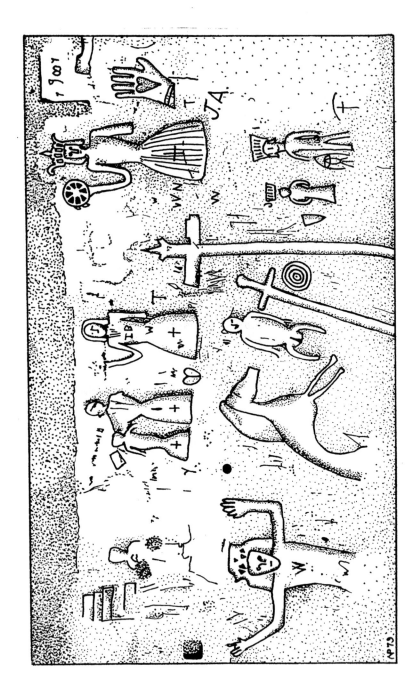

94

Chapter 12

The Cross Road

Because of its geomantic importance, sacred to the gods of flow, commerce, energy, fertility and the divine harmony, the crossroads has always been the site of ritual and performance, the favoured place for the foundation of new settlements. The cross road is important in West African religion, which parallels closely the practices and style of European Paganism. It appears also in North America in the tradition that underlies blues music, through which it has gained a significant meaning within contemporary western urban culture. This aspect of the crossroads as a place of interaction between the worlds is best expressed through the American legend that if someone wants to be a blues guitarist, he or she should take a guitar to the local crossroads at midnight. Then, a huge black man will appear, take the guitar, tune it, and play a piece on it. When the would-be musician gets the guitar back, he or she will be able to play the blues. Among others, the guitar virtuosi Robert Johnson and Jimi Hendrix are reputed to have gained their extraordinary powers of musicianship from this otherworldly

---

Fig. 29. Carvings in the Royston Cave, beneath the crossroads of the Icknield Way and Ermine Street at Royston in Hertfordshire. Archetypal principles are here represented in human form as the goddess with the Wheel Of Fortune (the personification of time, luck, fate and St Catherine), the sheela-na-gig (female sexuality) and other beings.

source. This supernatural black being at the crossroads is often identified with the Christian Devil by those unaware of nuances present in the African Pagan tradition of which it is part.

In the Yoruba tradition of West Africa, the god at the cross road is Eshu. His myths are recounted in the Yoruba divinatory text, *The Verses of the Sixteen Cowries*. In the Yoruba pantheon, the god Eshu, otherwise called Elégba or Júoriwà, is the divine messenger and trickster who serves the other goddesses and gods by rewarding humans who pray and sacrifice, disrupting the lives of those who offend or neglect their sacred duties. He is the youngest and most able of the deities created by Olorun, the god who rules over life and the destinies of humans and gods. Eshu has been described by William Bascom as "the divine enforcer" who dispenses godly justice, both rewarding and punishing. The god Orishala sent Eshu to live at the crossroads that is the image of all crossroads everywhere, and collect something from each passer-by. He did, and became wealthy and all-knowing by so doing, having no necessity to work. In West Africa, Eshu is acknowledged at every crossroads by a mud figure to which wayfarers offer pieces of food or cowrie shells. A traditional American blues song, that was recorded, *inter alia* by such blues luminaries as Robert Johnson, Homesick James and Eric Clapton, deals with this. The first verse of my favoured version is:

I went down to the cross road,
Fell down on my knees,
Went down to the cross road,
Fell down on my knees
Asked the lord above for mercy,
Save me if you please.

Whether we consider it from the standpoint of the in Greek, Roman, Nordic, English or Yoruba tradition, the crossroads is a place where the cosmic axis crosses the plane of Abred, the middle earth on which we walk. It is the place of the deity of change and flow, through which otherworldly influences may enter this world. In ancient Greece, the crossways was the *locus* of Hermes. To the Romans he was the god Mercury, and often a Herm was set up. This sacred structure was a stone pillar carved with an image of Hermes' head and genitalia. Frequently, a Herm would be accompanied by a tree and an altar upon which offerings would be made. An alternative dedication at the crossroads could be an altar to the four Celto-Roman goddesses of the four roads that run from the centre. The classical deity Hermes-Mercury is considered to be approximately equivalent with the Northern Tradition god Wotan-Woden-Odin, who is likewise the deity of the crossroads, the god of Hanged Men, among other attributes. In the Northern Tradition, it was customary to set up gallows or gibbets at crossroads, so that the spirits of the executed would pass rapidly down the cosmic axis into the underworld. The motif of death by hanging on a rope is also found in German labyrinth foundation-myths, and a West African legend of Eshu tells how the king of Igede sacrificed a knife to the god, which Eshu later used to cut the rope with which the king tried to hang himself.

In Britain, the display of the dismembered limbs and torsos of executed people at crossways continued until the eighteenth century. Certain national criminals, such as outlaws and highwaymen, executed in London, were cut into quarters and their parts displayed in the quarter-cities of England. According to this geomantic division, York represented the north; Cambridge the East; Hereford the west and Winchester the south. Oxford is the centre of this system, though there are several other claimants for the centre of England. I refer readers to John Michell's book *At the Centre of the World* for further discussion of this interesting matter of location. In the late seventeenth century, all over the west of England, the remains of prisoners-of-war executed after the Duke of Monmouth's army's defeat at Sedgemoor in 1685 were treated in this way on the orders of the hanging judge, Jeffreys. As well as displaying pieces of butchered humans, the crossroads were

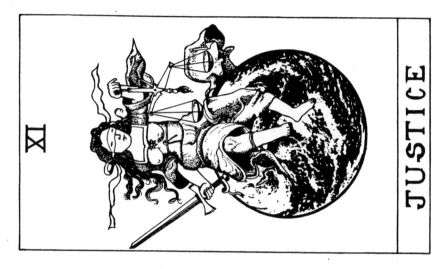

XI

JUSTICE

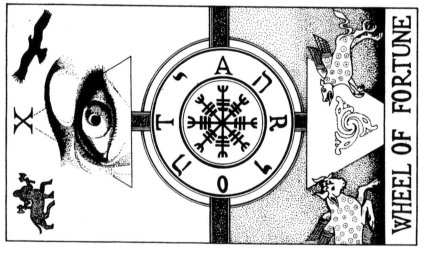

WHEEL OF FORTUNE

98

used for burying the bodies of those who, for some reason, did not qualify for burial in a Christian graveyard. In this way, the Nordic legend of Ymir was re-enacted: by tearing them apart and hanging them up at crossroads, the bodies of those who had not been taken from the world into the other, unworldly, system of Christianity, were returned to the earth.

Traitors, or those on the losing side in civil strife, were one such category of people to be buried at the cross road. For instance, the Chronicle of Roger of Wendover, records that in the mid-11th century, King Edward the Confessor ordered the burial of the traitor Godwin, thus: "Take forth this dog and traitor and bury him in a cross-way, for he is unworthy of Christian sepulture". Under English law, until 1823, it was directed that the body of a person who had taken her or his own life should be buried in a cross-road, and a stake driven through it. Other candidates for disposal in this manner were those executed as witches, heretics, highwaymen, outlaws, Romani and others whose presence in consecrated ground was considered undesirable. Sometimes, non-Christian and Romani people chose to be buried there rather than in ground claimed by a religion in which they had no faith.

Occasionally, these remains are unearthed to-day, when they are the cause of much puzzlement among local commentators unaware of the tradition. For example, during roadworks in the late 1970s, in the road now called the A14, several skeletons were found at the crossroads not far from Bar Hill where this is written. The bodies were buried unorientated, indicating that

---

Fig. 30.Tarot trumps X and XI from Nigel Pennick's *Way of the Eight Winds Tarot*. Major Arcanum X, *The Wheel of Fortune* is the epitome of the four elements and the eight directions, external and internal, from which come the fortunate and unfortunate events that shape our lives. Trump XI, *Justice* signifies the balance of opposites that composes existence, sitting on top of the world.

they were not Christian. The crossroads is the local high point, on a parish boundary where a straight Roman road aligned on Cambridge Castle mound crosses the local road system. It was also the site of a coaching inn, closed in the 1960s. These skeletons were a poignant reminder of the barbarousness of the historically quite recent past. After 1823, when Macadamised road surfaces and considerably increased traffic made things difficult, self-killers, nonconformists and executed criminals were allocated special unconsecrated cemeteries, though the Romani continued to use their own sacred plots away from the *gorgio* dead.

Crossroads are locally important sites, microcosmic images of the central navel of the world. That at Oxford, the Carfax, was taken by Welsh locators as the centre of Britain. The tower of St Martin's church marks the *omphalos* to-day. In the ancient British tradition, there are certain roads which came under the jurisdiction of the King's Peace - the Four Royal Roads of Britain. Ascribed to the British king Belinus, these four paved streets were confirmed by later, more historically-documented, monarchs as being under regal jurisdiction. These later kings included the penultimate Anglo-Saxon monarch, Edward the Confessor and the first Norman, William I, the Conqueror. Edward's roads were Watling Strete, Fosse, Hickenild Strete and Erming Strete. For some reason, William I only confirmed Watling, Erming and Fosse as being places under the King's Peace. As the whole length of each of these roads were special sanctuaries in themselves, the crossing-points were naturally very important *omphaloi*. Of the four crossings, three have a great historical importance: they are the centres of the towns of

---

Fig. 31. A medieval graffito of a hobby horse that can still be seen in the church at Girton, Cambridgeshire. It combines the wicker body and head of the traditional horse with the Northern Tradition tree of life.

Cirencester, Dunstable and Royston. The fourth, High Cross, near Leicester, is less significant for some reason, for a town was never constructed there. The four roads are also connected at two junction-points, in London and Lincoln. These are not crossways but locations with great cathedral sanctuaries. As earthly navels, Dunstable and Royston are the most important, though Cirencester possesses the appropriate cross for such a site.

The town of Dunstable was founded by King Henry I, and there is a documentary reference to a miracle play performed at Dunestaple in about the year 1115. Significantly, the play was an enactment of the Life of St Catherine, who, according to Christian mythology, was executed on a horizontal wheel on top of a post, symbolic of the cosmic axis. The *staple* element in the original name refers to an upright post, the cosmic axial pole that marked the crossing of the Royal Roads, extant before the town's foundation. The town of Dunstable itself as founded had the quartered 'Holy City' pattern with the streets named for the four directions (as in other such geomantic towns like Colchester, Oxford, Wareham and Chichester). At its centre was a stone cross. At a later date, one of the Eleanor Crosses was erected at the crossroads.

Chapter 13

The Pathway of Death: Crosses and Perrons

The finest stone crosses of English medieval art are the Eleanor Crosses. They were erected on the orders of Queen Eleanor's widower, King Edward I (a king known for his geomantic foundations), at the sites where her cortége halted on its journey from Harby in Nottinghamshire to Westminster, where she was buried in the Abbey. In his book, *Ancient Stone Crosses of England* (1875), Alfred Rimmer tells us that there were twelve Eleanor Crosses in all, at Lincoln, Grantham, Stamford, Geddington, Northampton, Stony Stratford, Woburn, Dunstable, St Alban's, Waltham, West Cheap and Charing. Twelve, of course, is a significant number of stages for a procession that marks the completion of a life. The last two crosses, West Cheap and Charing, are now in central London. The first was destroyed by Cromwell's soldiers, whilst the latter, Charing Cross, is now the central *omphalos* of the metropolis, from which distances are measured.

In keeping with the precise devotion to sacred ritual and geolocation practised by the locators of the time, each night the Queen's coffin rested on significant places of power. At Geddington, for example, the coffin rested at a place where later the Eleanor Cross was erected over a spring of clear water, a typical holy well which never ran dry. At Dunstable, the 'Lofty Cross' stood at the crossways. In mid-December, 1290, the locator, Prior Wederow, superintended the staking-out of the ground for the cross, and consecrated the site with holy water. It was erected under the supervision of John de Bello, who appears to have been the superintendent of cross-erection, at least at Dunstable, St Albans, Stony Stratford, Woburn and Northampton, if not all of them. Despite its brilliant workmanship, the Dunstable cross was destroyed as an 'idolatrous monument' in 1643 by fanatical Puritan Protestant militiamen commanded by the Earl of Essex.

In Hertfordshire, at Royston, the crossing of the Icknield Way and Ermine Street has no Eleanor Cross, but compensates for this by a most remarkable example of the Etruscan Discipline extant in England. Before modern changes, this crossroads was the meeting-point of five parishes and also the county boundary between Hertfordshire and Cambridgeshire. It has now been 'normalised', with the alteration of boundaries from their fascinatingly complex geomantic form to something that eases the task of the centralised bureaucrat. Over the years, similar gerrymandering of boundaries under the pressures of party politics and striving for simplicity has eliminated most of the geomantic niceties deemed necessary by the locators of old.

Royston, like Dunstable, has a royal connection befitting a cosmic centre. Dunstable had a royal palace used by Henry I, and Royston was patronised by a later king, James VI of Scotland/ I of England, whose residence was on the northbound road, to the north of the crossroads. Beneath the crossing is the unique Royston Cave, an octagonal-floored bottle-shaped structure cut in the clunch (chalk) bedrock. This is a true *mundus*, a subterranean image of the underworld whose walls are covered with carvings of the denizens of the world below, containing both Pagan and Christian symbolism. The remarkable images include a wheel-holding queen who is usually identified in line with Christian interpretations, as St Catherine, but equally can be seen as the Goddess of the Underworld, with her cosmic axial wheel. There is also a giant figure, who in the Christian interpretation signifies St Christopher, patron of roads and travelling, or according to the

Pagan view, Mercury, patron of the crossroads and travelling. Close by is a Sheela-na-gig whom the guides describe, prudishly and quite without reason, as the Christian-baiter Saul undergoing conversion to Christianity on the Road to Damascus; a horse, knights, several crucifixions, swords, hands and many other symbolic carvings of an even more enigmatical character. The figures appear to be in a naive sixteenth- or seventeenth-century style. Clearly, the *mundus* was used as some kind of sacred place in former times, though by whom and what for is unclear.

Ermine Street itself has a celestial connection, being identified with the Northern Tradition deity Irmin or Ing. Symbolically, he is the principle of eternal extension as the evolution of the microcosm, one of whose symbols is the cosmic-tree Irminsul. Ing is thus a further instance of the projection of the human onto the cosmos, and the Hermetic principle of "As above, so below". As a road on the surface of the earth, Ermine Street appears to be the earthly reflection of the celestial river of stars called the Milky Way, whose division into the two 'streams', called Wil and Wan echo the divergence of the two 'streets' of the four Royal Roads, Ermine Street and Watling Street. These two 'streets', Ermine and Watling run northwards and westwards, whilst the two 'ways', the Fosse and the Icknield, run eastwards and southwards. Such a complex yet logical melding of the symbolic and functional in one unified whole demonstrates the geomantic and organisational skills of the Roman *Agrimensores* who surveyed, planned and constructed them. Here, their geolocation shows a profound grasp of both mystic principles and sound transportation engineering, a masterly tribute to the Pagan education system which produced the locators of old - the Roman Agrimensores. The Royston Cave was sealed with a millstone, in accordance with the Etruscan Discipline. Symbolically, this is an allusion to the cosmic mill, whose static stone signifies ground-level between the heavens and the underworld.

106

The location of an Eleanor Cross at the intersection at Dunstable was a continuation of a tradition of the erection of a maypole, staple or tree at the *omphalos*. There is a clear transition from Pagan markers to Christian ones over the years, a gradual change characteristic of changing fashions rather than the religious revolution as some would portray it. In fact, the location of such markers never changed at all, and the symbolism was modified to accommodate the newer doctrines. The Gosforth Cross, a remarkable survival on several levels, displays this admirably, for, although of stone, its design reproduces tree bark and the form of the metal panels which once were attached by bolts to wooden staples. The Gosforth Cross has panels displaying elements from the Northern legend of the end of this worldly cycle, the last day, Ragnarök, and Christian mythology, on top of which is the wheel-cross used by Pagans and Christians alike.

Such crosses, of which several thousand fragments remain in the British Isles alone, had their own traditions of geolocation, orientation, iconography and liturgical colouring, most of which have been lost, or can be barely guessed at. A number of pre-conquest stone crosses still exist on their original sites, such as the Dane's Cross at Wolverhampton. Some are inserted in circular 'millstones', whilst others stand on steps, a representation of the cosmic holy mountain at the centre of the world. This stepped form, familiar from the Ziggurats of Mesopotamia, the pyramids of Mexico and the shrines of the Far East, is the local representation of the central mountain - Meru of the Hindus and Elbruz of the Mazdeans. Known as a Perron, these stepped bases sometimes reached enormous

---

Fig. 32. Mercury surmounting the globe, accompanied by his emblem, the serpent-twined *caduceus*, on which is the Hermetic winged helmet. The horns of plenty symbolize the riches that are to be found in the art of alchemy. From Cartari's *Le imagini de i dei*, 1581.

proportions. In South Wales, there are remarkable examples at Trelleck, Llantwit Major and St David's. At Winsford in Cheshire, the stepped base of the Perron contains a room formerly in use as a lock-up, parallelling the concept of Annwn.

But this steeped formation is not very common outside the context of Perron-crosses. The terraced law-mounds on which folk-moots once met, and upon which the Manx parliament still assembles to promulgate laws are part of this complex of related geomantic structures. It is also rare in church architecture, although the church of St Peter at Burgh St Peter in Suffolk has a much-patched-up tower which ascends stepwise to the heavens. Hawksmoor's famous eighteenth century church of St George at Bloomsbury in central London, has a stepped tower very similar to that supporting the Hercules statue erected on a high point and city/palace alignment near Kassel, Germany. These are both modelled on the Tomb of Mausolus, the Mausoleum, at Halicarnassus, which, as an entrance to the netherworld, was itself an image of the cosmos.

Fig. 33. A Celtic high cross from Bankhead, Forteviot parish, in Perthshire, Scotland, standing as guardian of the sacred trackway to the Holy Hill nearby. The emblematical scheme of carving shown here in 'exploded' form all over the cross is related not only to its symbolic position on the cross itself, but to its cosmological meaning on a wider level.

MYN GLAS LOOPT RAS

110

Chapter 14

The Path of the Serpent

According to Northern Tradition symbolic cosmology, the cosmic axis is surrounded by the world serpent, Jörmungand or Niöhöggr, which encompasses the axis in a manner similar to that of a turf labyrinth about a central marker. This image is expressed well upon a Greek altar in the British Museum, where a serpent is coiled around it. Symbolically, the serpent around the axis represents the tension between stability and fluidity. The cosmic axis is a symbol of eternal stability, standing steady while all else shakes and breaks up. The serpent, on the other hand, symbolises ever-moving, unfixed, energy. The two are the opposite ends of the Druidic cosmos - *Calas* and *Nwyvre*. When the two are together, we have a symbol of the active process that must be enacted for existence to proceed on the material level. If there is nothing but structure without energy, then all is at a standstill - there is stasis Conversely, if there is nothing but energy without structure, there is chaos. Only when the opposites are brought together can the multiple patterns of existence proceed. This is

---

Fig. 34. The skull is the most recognizably human of the remains left after the decay of the flesh from the corpse. Here, in a 17th century Dutch engraving, "Myn Glas Loopt Ras" means "My (hour) glass runs fast", that is, time flies. Here, it stands as a *memento mori*. As a symbol of death, the skull and crossbones was the emblem of pirates, the Nazi SS, members of the the Ancient Order of Bonesmen and others who dealt out death or in some way handled the remains of the human dead.

expressed in the Norse creation myth by the coming-together of ice and fire in the Yawning Gap of nothingness.

The coiling serpent image is well expressed mythically in the Northumbrian legend of the Lambton Worm, where a serpent coils around a rock or hillock, impressing its patterns into the side, making it into an image of the stepped Perron, like Glastonbury Tor. This image can also be seen at several of the surviving ancient European turf labyrinths. It is known that in former times, some of them actually had trees or stones at their centres. The biggest ancient turf labyrinth, in the Eilenriede Forest at Hannover in Germany, has a large linden tree at its centre. Similarly, the former maze of the Shoemakers' Guild at Stolp in Pomerania had a tree at its centre in 1784 when the now-famous engraving of it was made.

In England, an ash tree once stood at the centre of the Saffron Walden (Essex) maze. Unfortunately, this was destroyed by fire on Guy Fawkes' Night in 1823, coincidentally the year that crossroads burial was officially discontinued. An attempt a few

---

Fig. 35. Masonic, tradesmen's, personal and magical stave sigils of the medieval and renaissance periods from East Anglia. Top row: 1. Long Melford; 2 and 3. Great Saxham; 4. Hintlesham; 5. Hitcham; 6. Great Waldingfield; 7. Framlingham; 8. Nayland. Second row: 1. Bury St Edmunds; 2. Woolpit; 3. Robert Lucas; 4. Ixworth; 5. Richard Martyn; 6. Thomas Fygott; 7. Robert Hwell. Third line: 1. Awall, Grundisborough, 1510, showing the '4' sigil of Mercury, the tradesmen's guardian; 2. Richard Martyn, Ipswich, 1621; 3. Thomas Awall, salter, Grundisborough, 1530; 4. Myghell Fox, Chacombe, 1500; 5. Christian Merrell, Ipswich, 1600; 6. John Cage. Line four: 1. John Berffe, Brightlingsea, 1521; 2. Robert Weeks; 3. Christopher Grayne; 4.John Beaumont; 5. John Clerk; 6. John Bronde; 7. Anthony Meryman. Line five: 1. Lowestoft; 2. Thomas Cole; 3. Combs; 4. John James; 5. The Ipswich Warding Sign; 6. William Sandy, the *wolfsangel*; 7. John Deken, Ipswich, 1434; 8. John Dekens, Ipswich, 1419. Line six: 1. Sudbury; 2. Hitcham; 3. Brettenham; 4 - end, masons' marks, King's College Chapel, Cambridge. Line 7: Masons' marks, King's College Chapel, Cambridge, 1446 - 1515.

years ago to get a new tree planted was blocked at the last minute. A tree grows at the centre of the enormous labyrinth in Willen Park at Milton Keynes. Other labyrinths once snaked around central markers. The now-obliterated turf labyrinth at Horncastle in Lincolnshire had a stone cross at its centre, and the existing 'maze' at Hilton has at its centre a monument erected to the memory of William Sparrow, who cut the labyrinth at the time of the restoration of King Charles II. Both the trees and the stones are yet further aspects of the cosmic axis.

Overall, there are two related but distinct themata associated with the cosmic axis. The first is the cosmic axis as a spiritual model, a method of envisaging or explaining the phenomena encountered in the journeys of the soul, within and without the body. The second is a group of phenomena associated with the physical geolocation of an object, which is the worldly image or reflexion of the eternal cosmic reality. The ancient secret brotherhoods and mysteries from which survive the Freemasons as an organisation, and knowledge of the inner workings of a few others, such as The Society of the Horseman's Word, The Ancient Order of Bonesmen and the Guild of Hammermen, used oaths which bound their members to secrecy. Today, in an age when a man's word is frequently untrustworthy, and honour has no place in the cut-throat world of big business, the secrets of the Masons, the Horsemen and Wicca have been published for all to see, and probably to mock. But the revelation of the outward form is not necessarily the revelation of essence, and theory without practice is nothing. It is through direct experience under proper guidance that people can encounter the true realities expressed in the secret teachings, the power of special places, and the Elder Faith.

Chapter 15

The Labyrinth

All attempts to classify anything in the world are full of dangers. Nature is infinitely diverse, and attempts to bring human order to its essentially continuous structure are bound to be only partly successful. Even with the products of the human mind, classification may not be as easy as if at first appears. This is the case with labyrinths. As defined here, a labyrinth is an artificial pattern that compresses a path into a small space. It is unicursal, that is, there is only one path, without dead ends, which brings one from the outside to the centre (and perhaps back out again). Labyrinths can take many forms, but historically, there has been a development from simpler to more complex forms. There is a remarkable versatility in labyrinth patterns; throughout history, each type of labyrinth has appeared in many variant forms. Excitingly, the labyrinth is being developed still, enjoying a renaissance in the post-modern era.

The labyrinth is a unique human artifact, for it remains recognisable in whatever form it may appear. It can be made small, as in a jewel, or large enough to walk through. Walkable labyrinths have been made of stones, cut in the turf, formed of mosaic stones, delineated by hedges or painted on tarmac. However they are made, they produce certain psychological effects in the walker, which can prove transformative under the right conditions. Symbolically, the labyrinth is transcendental. Its has deep meaning in Mediterranean Paganism, the Northern Tradition, Hinduism, Afghan legend, Jewish mythical

LABYRINTH CONSTRUCTION

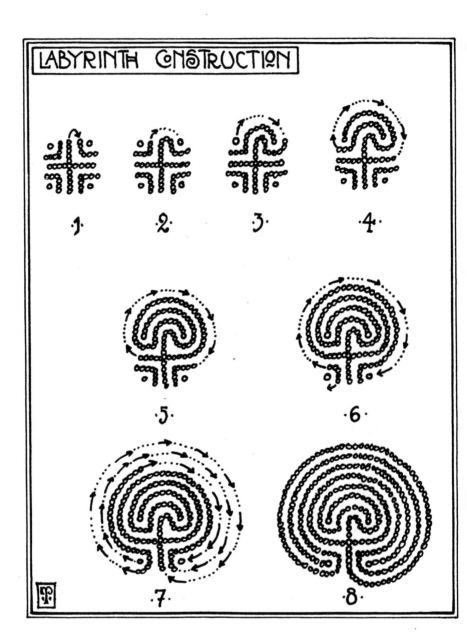

·1·　　·2·　　3·　　·4·

·5·　　　　·6·

·7·　　　　·8·

history and Christian symbolism of both the Orthodox and Catholic branches. It is the City of Troy, the House of Wayland, Jericho, Solomon's Palace, Jerusalem, Nineveh, Shamaili's House, The Fortress, The Virgin's Dance, Julian's Bower.....the list is almost endless, for the labyrinth remains a living force, with new names coming into being appropriate to new conditions as they arise.

The Classical Labyrinth

The Classical Labyrinth is a version of the ancient meander-pattern. Often, it is called the Cretan Labyrinth from its use on coins from Knossos and their allusion to the labyrinth of Daedalus. This labyrinth form may have originated independently in several places, or may have been transmitted from one origin-point. It is known in ancient northern Europe as well as the Caucasus, India and north America. Perhaps it arose from the recesses of the mind, discovered in shamanic flights of the mind, or the geometrical experiments of craftsmen and women. Whichever mystery gave birth to the labyrinth, in its brilliant simplicity it retains its magic to this day.

Geometrically, the Classical Labyrinth can be drawn from what is called the cross, corners and dots pattern. This pattern is the fourfold version of a general principle (rarely used historically), that allows labyrinths to be made with any number of corners and dots. The cross, corners and dots pattern is linked structurally with the nine-dot-pattern that underlies the Fylfot and the Shield-Knot. Like the labyrinth, they are sigils that protect against harm. These sigils show the principle of analogous forms which characterises the European magical tradition.

Fig. 36. The technique of construction of the classical labyrinth, starting from the cross, corners and dots pattern.

The Classical Labyrinth can take a left-handed or right-handed turn by the entrance. Most modern ones have a right-hand entrance, perhaps the result of universal literacy. The Classical Labyrinth has another kind of variation. Its basic form has seven walls, but there is also a more developed form, with more walls, derived from a basal pattern with two or more 'corners' before the 'dots'. The best-known ancient examples of this form are the stone labyrinth at Visby on the island of Gotland, Sweden, and the privately-owned turf one at Troy Farm at Somerton in Oxfordshire, England.

Another version of the Classical Labyrinth is a unicursal one that allows exit without retracing one's steps. This is known historically from the Baltic and German-speaking regions. In its simplest form, it is derived easily from the standard Classical form, although it may have derived from simpler, back-and-forth spiral types, such as one which once existed at Rockcliffe Marsh in Cumbria. Whatever its origin, it can be constructed from an expanded version of the cross, corners and dots pattern which has two parallel lines at the centre, which gives a parallel entrance and exit. Other versions of this labyrinth have a spiral centre. This type of labyrinth was favoured by the German athletic movement in the middle of the 19th century, when traditional designs were used on new sites. Practically, it allows great freedom in labyrinth-running when many people participate at once.

The Roman Labyrinth

Like the Classical Labyrinth, the Roman form is derived from the meander-pattern. Roman labyrinths are known almost exclusively from mosaic pavements. Here, the labyrinth is divided into four quarters, each a meander-pattern (or sometimes two or more). The path is simple. It visits each quarter in turn, tracing the whole quarter before passing on to the next. All four quarters are visited in turn before the centre is reached. Roman labyrinths may be square or round. Rarely, other more embellished forms were made, the models for later medieval labyrinths in churches. Some Roman mosaic labyrinths were big enough to walk through, whilst others served a more decorative and magical function, being as small as a metre in diameter. The themes of the besieged central city, such as Troy, or the Cretan fable of Theseus and the Minotaur were used often in or around these pavement labyrinths.

Medieval Labyrinths

The Medieval European Labyrinth is derived from the Roman form. It retains the four quarters of its predecessor, but adds the facility of crossing-over from quarter to quarter at various points. This gives a much more interesting and sometimes surprising pathway. The Roman labyrinth is clearly its origin, for, through historical examples, it can be seen tending towards the medieval form by way of transitional forms. A good example of this is the surviving late classical labyrinth at Kato Paphos in Cyprus, where additional paths are added to the standard Roman labyrinth pattern on the inside and outside. The mosaic labyrinth in the 6th century church of San Vitale at the Gothic capital of Italy, Ravenna, is an early developed form of the Roman labyrinth. Like the Roman labyrinth, the medieval form is divided into four quarters, but, unlike the standard Roman form, the paths cross back and forth between the quarters.

Another version of medieval labyrinth is the so-called Otfrid-pattern. This is a development of the Classical Labyrinth which has many intricate turnings, but no quartered form. It is named after the priest Otfrid von Weissenburg (c.790-875), who taught in Alsace at a time when abbeys were being founded according to geomantic omens. The Otfrid form was also used by medieval Jewish scribes, who described it as being the city of Jericho. Strangely, it does not exist as a historic walkable labyrinth. The most publicised medieval labyrinth of all is in the cathedral at Chartres in France, constructed around the year 1220, which many people take as the definitive 'Christian'

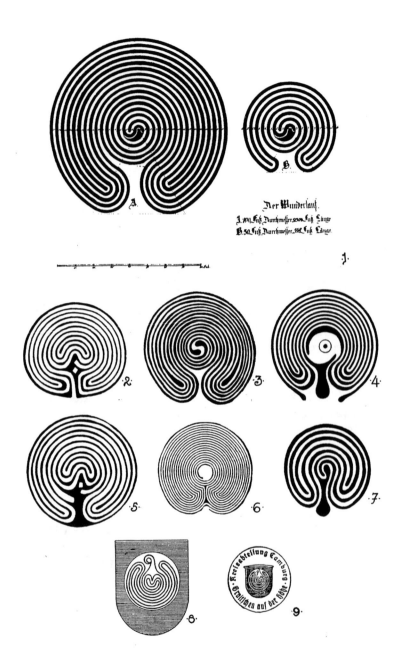

Der Wunderlauf.

A. 100 Fuß Durchmesser 2500 Fuß Länge
B. 50 Fuß Durchmesser 600 Fuß Länge.

labyrinth. Its pattern is the same as that of the earlier labyrinth incised on a cathedral pillar at Lucca in Italy. When built, the Chartres labyrinth contained symbolic elements from three religions. At the centre was the Minotaur of Mediterranean Paganism; in the path was a Jewish quotation about the walls of Jerusalem (Psalm 51); the whole labyrinth represented the Christian concept of the road to salvation. The transcendent nature of the labyrinth as a manifestation of the Perennial Philosophy that cuts across religious boundaries is nowhere more apparent than here. In pre-Christian times, Chartres was one of the chief centres of Druidism in Gaul, and the labyrinth is a place of pilgrimage to-day for the Romani of western Europe.

But the medieval labyrinth is far more ranging in form than just the Chartres form, which differs from others in having a 7-fold centre. Almost every known medieval church labyrinth was in some way different from that at Chartres. Some have the same path-form, but have large or small centres. There are both right- and left-handed pathways. In France, large circular church labyrinths existed at *inter alia* Bayeux, Poitiers and Sens, all of which had patterns different from the Chartres labyrinth. Some turf mazes in England had a similar path-form to the Chartres labyrinth, whilst others did not. Centre-patterns included spirals running both ways and loops which turned the walker round to come out again.

The octagonal forms of the labyrinth and designs with corner-pieces are significant sub-forms of the medieval labyrinth. The

---

Fig. 37. The German labyrinth tradition. 1. *Wunderläufe,* from W. Lübeck, 1843-4. 2. Steigra; 3. Kaufbeuren, Bavaria (destroyed 1942); 3. Eilenriede Forest, Hanover; 4. Graitschen; 6. Labyrinth of the Shoemakers' Guild, Stolp, Pomerania (Stupsk, Poland, destroyed c. 1945); 7. Dransfeld (destroyed 1957); 8. Municipal arms of Graitschen; 9. Municipal seal of Graitschen.

best known of these are also French church pavement labyrinths from Arras, Amiens, St-Quentin and Reims. Again, like their circular counterparts, these had significant variations. The octagonal labyrinth at Amiens, built in 1288, called "The House of Daedalus" served as the model for one at St-Quentin (1495). The labyrinth at Reims had yet a different pattern of pathway, with corner 'bastions', and yet another pattern was laid in a church at Sélestat in 1875. A version of this, on a circular basis, exists in the turf labyrinth at Saffron Walden in Essex. Another, with yet a different pathway, existed before 1797 at Sneinton in Nottinghamshire. This one was associated with Robin Hood.

A quite different type of medieval labyrinth is that originally laid at the Abbey of St-Bertin at St-Omer, in Pas-de-Calais, France. A version of this was laid out in Gent, in Flanders, Belgium in 1533, and, more recently, in the church at Batheaston in the county of Avon, made in 1985. Its strictly rectilinear design is yet another variation on the theme. Other forms include the enigmatic labyrinth in Frankfurt cathedral, Germany, and the turf labyrinth at St Catherine's Hill at Winchester in Hampshire, which is a rounded square.

The nineteenth century saw a renewed interest in labyrinths, when architects designed new pavement labyrinths to the medieval design. In the 1850s, a copy of the St-Quentin labyrinth was built at the church of Notre-Dame-de-la-Treille at

---

Fig. 38. Traditional labyrinth patterns: 1. The classical labyrith, with 7 rings; 2. Classical labyrinth with 11 rings. Turf labyrinth at Troy Farm at Somerton in Oxfordshire; 3. Sixth century pavement labyrinth in the church of San Vitale in Ravenna, Italy; 4. Pavement labyrinth in Chartres Cathedral, c. 1220; 5. Pavement labyrinth formerly in Sens Cathedral, France (destroyed 1769); 6. Turf labyrinth on Ripon Common, Yorkshire (destroyed in 19th century); 7. Turf labyrinth at Marfleet, Holderness, Yorkshire (destroyed in 19th century); 8. Shoemakers' Guild labyrinth formerly at Kingsland, Shrewsbury (destroyed in 19th century).

124

Lille in northern France; in 1866, a circular 'medieval' labyrinth was laid in the church at Itchen Stoke in Hampshire; in 1870, Sir Gilbert Scott's labyrinth at Ely in Cambridgeshire was laid, with a path length equal to the height of the cathedral tower beneath which it lies. At Sélestat, Alsace (now France, then Germany), an octagonal labyrinth was laid in the church of St Fides around 1875. This is surrounded by emblems of the 'four rivers of the world'. In Wales, another octagonal labyrinth designed by William Burges was laid in the Chaucer Room at Cardiff Castle. The Amiens labyrinth, destroyed in 1828, was reinstated in 1894, and Mary Tytler Watts incorporated labyrinths into her symbolic chapel at Compton in Surrey, as symbolic of "The Way". The author's book, *Mazes and Labyrinths* (Robert Hale, 1990) contains a much more detailed and comprehensive treatment of these and other allied labyrinthine themes.

Aquarian Labyrinths

The present Aquarian Age (or Postmodern Era) is characterised by the breakdown of the structures that had become established over the previous 200 years by industrialisation and the resultant centralised political systems. The disintegration of established religion, the downgrading of the environment through pollution, the breakdown of industrial economics, the devastating effects of war, mass migrations of people and a revolution in information technology are transforming the character of the world. This 'New Age' has seen a remarkable reinstatement of many ancient traditions, hitherto thought of as extinct. Some are of great spiritual value, whilst others (according to the law of the unity of opposites) have brought mayhem and murder in the name of millennarianism. But in general, esoteric thought has

Fig. 39. The labyrinth: place of spirit.

undergone a remarkable renaissance, empowered by information and techniques from all parts of the Earth.

This renaissance has seen us reclaim the ancient skills and wisdom of the indigenous European spiritual tradition. The Elder Faiths of Europe, long suppressed, have been restored; their traditions reinstated; their scriptures and pantheons recognised again as a valuable heritage which can make a fresh contribution to Western Civilisation. The restoration of the labyrinth is an indication of the psychic change that this 'New Age' may represent. As a symbol of Mother Earth, the labyrinth has taken on a new vitality, expressing recognition of our human dependence upon the Earth, reverence for the female principle in life, and hope for a future when the ancient respect for the Earth will be restored once more.

Chapter 16

The Divine Harmony, Proportion and Symbolism

The Pagan civilisation of ancient Greece is noted for its pioneering and experimental approach towards the world. Intellectually, ancient Greek thought lies at the basis of modern European civilisation as it exists now. Numerous philosophers set up theories which others disputed and discussed with reasoned argument and practical experiment. In this heady milieu, where no overall dogma was imposed from above by the state, many important discoveries were made and insights obtained.

Among this burgeoning of human knowledge was a teaching by Pythagoras in the late sixth century BCE, concerning the principles of the divine harmony, expressed in its earthly form as music. He noted that on a musical instrument, tuned strings sound in harmony when their lengths are related to one another by certain whole-number measurements. Pythagoras had made the radically-important discovery that musical tones can be measured in terms of space. For instance, if two strings vibrate under the same conditions, one being half the length of the other, the pitch of the shorter string will be a *diapason* (octave) above that of the longer one. If the strings are arranged in a length-ratio of 2:3, then the difference in pitch will be a *diapente* (fifth), and if the ratio of length is 3:4, then the difference will be a *diatessaron* (fourth). Thus, these consonances of Pythagoras are expressed in the simple progression 1:2:3:4, which contains in addition to *diapason, diatessaron* and *diapente,* octave-and-a-fifth, 1:2:3; and two octaves, 1:2:4.

When this brilliant discovery was re-publicised in the sixteenth century, it came to from the basis of the harmonic systems used in European architecture of the Renaissance and later periods. The discovery of Pythagoras was viewed in terms of a divine revelation of the universal harmony inherent in all things. Now the whole universe could be explained in terms of mathematics. In order to achieve mastery of this universe, claimed the Pythagoreans, it was necessary for human beings to discover the numbers that are hidden within all things. The revival of this doctrine twenty-two centuries after its first exposition was responsible for the expansive development of science which has re-shaped the world into its present condition.

The Pythagoreans asserted that numbers were in some way independent things that possessed certain indivisible and eternal spatial dimensions. However, despite this theory, they were intelligent and practical enough to recognise that, for instance, the diagonals of squares are not measurable in terms of whole units. Pythagoras called such 'numbers' *measureless.* Later, such 'numbers' as the square root of three were to be termed *irrational,* that is, inexpressible in terms of measure. As it was expressed, this Pythagorean concept of things being composed of finite units was soon criticised by the Stoic philosopher, Zeno, who, by means of his famous *paradox,* discredited the theory. Pythagoras claimed that these numbers, their ratios and proportions were fundamental to the entire fabric of the world. Amid these figures, the cube was seen as the culminating perfection, for in classical, physical, geometry, it is impossible to progress beyond the third dimension of length, width and height.

James Fergusson, in his *A History of Architecture in All Countries,* commented on Greek mystical mathematics in general, "The system of definite proportion which the Greeks employed in the design of their temples, was another cause of the effect they produce even on uneducated minds. It was not with them merely that the height was equal to the width, or the length about twice the breadth; but every part was proportioned to all those parts to which it related, in some such ratio as 1 to 6, 2 to 7, 3 to 8, 4 to 9, or 5 to 10, etc. As the scheme advances, these numbers become undesirably high. In this case, they reverted to some such simple ratio as 4 to 5, 5 to 6, 6 to 7, and so on."

This system of proportionality is nowhere as apparent as in the Athenian Parthenon. This wonderful Pagan temple, now ruined, was constructed as a replacement for a smaller temple also dedicated to the goddess Athena on the same site. The earlier structure had been destroyed by the Persian military in 480 BCE. Because it had been built on the foundations of an earlier temple which itself had superseded a Mycenaean Throne Room, the Parthenon was laid out according to the old Mycenaean system of measure rather than the then current Greek Foot. But the major dimensions were chosen so carefully that they were 'round figures' in both Mycenaean Feet and Greek Feet, which measures are related in the ratio 10:9.

The sacred geometry of the Parthenon was such that it incorporated significant symbolic measures. These dimensions were recorded meticulously by an English architect, Francis Cranmer Penrose, who measured the temple to a precision of one-thousandth of an English foot (0.3mm). Penrose determined that the Parthenon had not been laid out with perfectly straight lines, but instead had utilised subtle mathematical curves in its fabric. Thus, the Parthenon represents another order of sacred geometry, something quite out of the ordinary. In addition, Penrose determined that there are some essential similarities between the geometrical structure of the Parthenon and the Great Pyramid. The elevations of the Parthenon's fronts were determined by Golden Section geometry, and the sides were based upon the factor π. In addition to Penrose's discoveries, Professor Steccini has shown that some slight

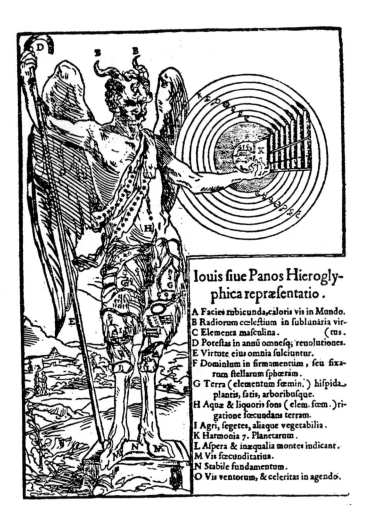

Iouis siue Panos Hierogly-
phica repræsentatio.

A Facies rubicunda, caloris vis in Mundo.
B Radiorum cœlestium in sublunaria vir-
C Elementa masculina.   (tus.
D Potestas in annū omnesq; reuolutiones.
E Virtute eius omnia fulciuntur.
F Dominium in firmamentūm , seu fixa-
    rum stellarum sphœrám.
G Terra (elementum fœmin.) hispida,
    plantis, satis, arboribusque.
H Aquæ & liquoris fons (elem. fœm.) ri-
    gatione fœcundans terram.
I Agri, segetes, aliaque vegetabilia .
K Harmonia 7. Planetarum.
L Aspera & inæqualia montes indicant .
M Vis fœcunditatius.
N Stabile fundamentum.
O Vis ventorum, & celeritas in agendo.

deviations in the base of the Parthenon were deliberate and not the result of miscalculations on the part of the geometers. In his view, the ø to π relationship of end-to-side in the Parthenon parallels that of the north face of the Great Pyramid (ø) to the west face (π).

In addition to these geometrical ratios, the width of the fronts of the Parthenon were such as to indicate a second of degree at the equator. By incorporating such measure, the individual parts of the fabric, each proportioned commensurably with the basic geometrical form of the whole edifice, were in turn proportioned with regard to the dimensions of the Earth herself.

The divine harmoniousness thus engendered immediately integrates the construction with the cosmos. Integrated with the overall harmony of existence, it is thereby a perfect vessel for worship, which aims to integrate the human with the divine. The threefold necessities for a functional temple - orientation, geometry and measure - are present in the Parthenon and in every other truly sacred building planted on the Earth. This degree of integration is attainable by no other method.

Following on from Pythagorean number lore, Plato, in his *Timaeus,* asserted that the cosmic harmony is contained within certain numbers formed in the squares of the double and triple proportion commencing at unity. These are created by the two geometrical progressions 1,2,4,8 and 1,3,9,27. Traditionally represented in the form of the Greek letter Lambda, λ, they

---

Fig. 40. The seven notes of the *syrinx or* Pipes of Pan, instrument of the Great God Pan, reproduce the music of the spheres of the seven planets of traditional astrology. Like each human being, the Great God Pan is the epitome of all things, containing in his constitution all of existence.

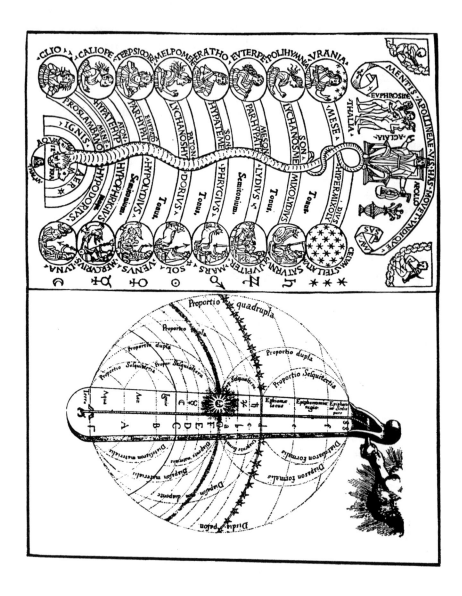

pervade the European geometrical tradition from ancient Greece to the modern age.

To Plato, the harmony of the universe was expressed in seven numbers. (Seven in itself is a mystical number, being the number of planets in pre-Copernican astronomy, reflected, *inter alia*, in the seven notes of the Octave, the Seven Wonders of the World, the Seven Patriarchs of Judaism, the Seven Pious Ones of the World, the Seven Sacraments of the Roman Catholic Church and the Seven Champions of Christendom). These numbers are 1,2,3,4,8,9 and 27, figures that encompass the mysteries of macrocosm and microcosm, symbolic numbers suited, above all others, for incorporation in sacred architecture.

In his prescription for the foundation of a new city, Plato asserted that each and every detail necessitated the closest consideration. His plan took into account his ideals in terms of the numbers, geometry, geolocation and social factors of life in a city. He recommended that the temples should be arranged around a marketplace and also throughout the city on high points. The geometrical nature of the city's plan, like those of ancient Greece in general, was taken for granted. Its location and geomantic design was to be regulated by an Urban Commission empowered to regulate alterations and to prohibit changes which would alter the overall scheme. The design which was to govern the city was held to be essential for the

---

Fig. 41. The Divine Harmony and the Music of the Spheres. Left: Under the rulership of Apollo, whose stringed instrument complements the Pipes of Pan, the modes of music are ruled by the Muses and the planets, linked by the three-headed Nwyvre to the four elements of which they are composed. Right: the cosmos symbolized as a finely-tuned musical instrument containing the geometrical proportions that define the musical notes, thereby distinguishing harmony from discord, which again is related to the planets and elements of classical spirituality.

happiness of its inhabitants. Plato believed that people would never know happiness until the designers of their cities were artists who took the pattern of the divine as their plan.

This divine pattern, as enumerated in Plato's *Republic*, was a cosmological schema that served as a microcosm of the divine harmony. In such an ideal plan, even the number of inhabitants of the city should conform to the harmonic mean. Thus, Plato recommended that there should be 5040 landholders, each occupying his own plot of land. This number is typical, for it is one that is almost universally divisible. It is derived from the multiplication of the numbers 1 to 7, and consequently is divisible by all of the numbers from 1 to 10 as well as 12.

The whole country surrounding the acropolis of Plato's ideal city was to be divided twelvefold, but equal opportunities were to be ensured by an ingenious provision whereby allotments of less productive land should be proportionately larger than those on fertile soil. Of course, in practice, this would be a difficult, if not impossible, undertaking. But the *Republic* was an allegorical microcosm in every sense. Its geometrical and numerological attributes were all chosen to demonstrate a divine ideal, the consummation of which, if realised, would render human beings at one with the universe - the final goal throughout history of the esoteric sciences.

Chapter 17

Medieval Sacred Symbolism

The great medieval churches of Europe are the finest flowering of the art of sacred symbolism that still stand intact on this continent. Like the great classical Pagan temples before them, they are the physical manifestations of the *Summa Theologiae*, designed specifically as the microcosmic embodiment of the created universe. In their perfect completeness these holy buildings united in their form the appropriate qualities of location, orientation, geometry, proportion and symbolic content. They have been seen by some esotericists as remarkably successful attempts by the operative freemasons to complete the *Great Work*, whose goal is the unification of the human with the divine. Because of this, the medieval church buildings were not designed merely as functional sheds with the purpose of accommodating a certain number of worshippers; neither, as has often been inferred by those who should know better, were they built 'as they went along'.

From ancient Egypt onwards, every large building has been the result of sophisticated technical planning involving accurate measuring, parameteric and geometrical drawings. Just as in modern architectural practice, everything in ancient times was also worked out in advance to the last detail. Each and every feature of the building was determined precisely. Surviving records show the absolute professionalism of the honourable masters who designed and supervised the construction of these medieval sacred buildings. Among these records are the exquisite working drawings for the elevation of the west front of the cathedral at Strasbourg and alternative designs for the spire at Ulm Minster.

Many of the great European churches, including St Peter's at Rome and the cathedrals or abbeys at Bamberg, Bath, Compostela, Chartres, Nîmes, Paris, Peterborough, Glasgow, Speyer, Upsala and Vilnius were built on the sites of places of former Pagan sanctity. In turn, these locations had been chosen earlier because of their numinous qualities, so that they might employ to the best effect any telluric energies perceived to be present there. Many of these churches stand at places where standing stones once stood. When the first churches were erected there, the stones of the old religion were used in the foundations or walls of the new building. It is possible that in some places, the symbolic sacred geometry of the stones was reflected in that of the new church.

Speculating literalistically, the French researcher Louis Charpentier has suggested that the stones in these ancient megalithic structures, in addition to absorbing cosmic and telluric influences, served as instruments of vibration. These stone 'instruments', he claims, could accumulate and amplify the vibrations present at these sites, acting in the manner of a resonant drum. These energies, as valuable to the Christian clergymen as to the Pagan priests and priestesses before them, still required a resonator, and this, according to Charpentier, was provided by the stone walls and vaulting of the church.

This rather materialistic, para-scientific, interpretation of divine-harmonic geometry seems appropriate for modern, technologically-orientated, tastes. It remains to be seen whether this theory has any scientific evidence to back it up. It is certain, however, that the appropriate use of harmonic proportion in a building does enhance its acoustical properties, and hence a geometry based on Pythagorean principles will prove useful. But Charpentier claims also that the Benedictine monks somehow amplified telluric energies by means of physical sound, specifically in Gregorian Chant. This action, enhanced by the building's geometry, is claimed to produce enhanced states of consciousness within the participants. It really is a notable feature of these great buildings that inside one may experience an altered consciousness.

Inevitably, terrestrial phenomena within and outside sacred buildings have been and will continue to be interpreted according to the cultural fashions of the era: trolls, spirits, fairies, devils, yarthkins, angels, the Madonna, magnetism, odyle, underground water, radio waves, electrostatic forces, unknown energies, 'e-leys', orgone, devas, deros, extra-terrestrial beings, and whatever comes next in this continuing unfolding of belief-claims. Whilst dealing with all subjective, symbolic, responses to the earth, it is important above all else to remain conscious so as not to fall into the trap of taking literally these glimpses of other things. Furthermore, as researchers of the esoteric, we should always retain our awareness of the possibility of making fresh insights and correcting former errors of observation and interpretation.

In any field of human endeavour, those who fail to exercise their creative and critical faculties are fated to sink into fundamentalism, claiming the untenable doctrine that, in ancient times, absolute, immutable truth was revealed, and that because of this, the present can make no contribution other than to follow the past slavishly. But, since the Megalithic period at least, this has not been the European way: in the 19th century, the great French magus Éliphas Lévi expressed this significantly: "We study tradition, but we do not consider it to be a critical authority, for it is the common receptacle of antiquity's errors as well as its truth." If we perpetuate ideas or concepts that have been modified or disproved, then we abdicate any opportunity that our wyrd has given us to contribute to human progress.

Whatever the truth of twentieth-century energy-theories which take the technology of power generation and transmission as their models, it is certain that the various elements of the

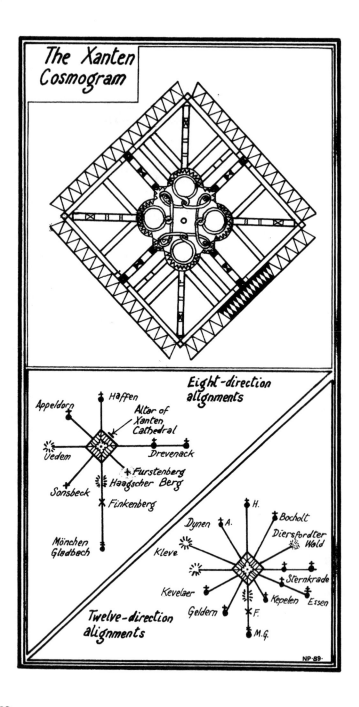

The Xanten Cosmogram

Eight-direction alignments

Haffen
Appeldorn
Altar of Xanten Cathedral
Uedem
Drevenack
Furstenberg
Haagscher Berg
Sonsbeck
Finkenberg
Mönchen Gladbach

Twelve-direction alignments

Dynen
H.
A.
Bocholt
Diersfordter Wold
Kleve
Sternkrade
Kevelaer
Kepelen
Essen
Geldern
F.
M.G.

NP·89·

larger late medieval churches were harmonised to create a whole that linked the human microcosmic being with the universe at large. The masons brought the music of the spheres from the cosmos down to earth and froze it in stone: as it was above, so it was below. The multiple functions that the builders and users of the cathedrals expected meant that they could not be relatively simple expressions of basic geometries like Saint-Chapelle in Paris or King's College Chapel in Cambridge. Cathedrals needed various divisions and subdivisions set aside from one another to service the functions of meeting-place, parish church, chantry, confessional and allow the ceremonies associated with the office of bishop. In addition to these exoteric uses, the cathedral had to embody the doctrines of the faith current at the time of construction, and also express the qualities inherent in the place, emanating from the *anima loci*. Because of these requirements, the geometrical bases of many late medieval cathedrals embody may complex structures which may be interpreted on a number of levels.

In such a building, the fundamental geometry is always generated directly from the orientated axial centre-line. The technique of orientation in Christian churches is derived from the practices of the augurs in the Etruscan Discipline, preserving aspects of earlier cults that venerated the Sun, such as Egyptian religion. Traditionally orientated churches, therefore, are aligned generally towards sunrise on the day dedicated to the patron saint. This means that as long as the church stands, the date and position of the original foundation is preserved in this axis, and hence in all of the geometrical

---

Fig. 42. This mosaic pavement cosmogram at Xanten Cathedral in the Rhineland of Germany, was found by the geomantic researcher Josef Heinsch to be a symbolic diagram that related the inner geometry of the church to the outer geometry of the landscape. Thus, the diagram is a conceptual model of the landscape, in which the outer is reflected in the inner in a form of parameteric diagram.

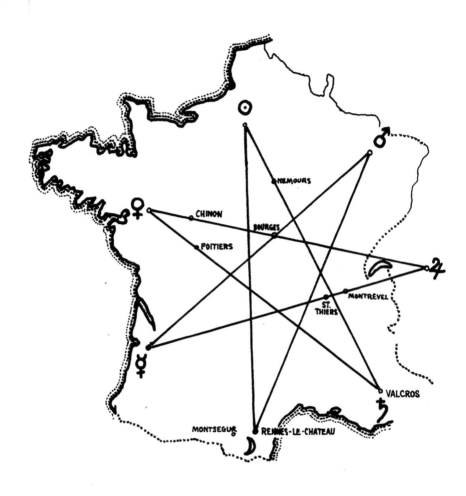

relationships derived from it. Thus, on each successive patronal day, the sun would shine directly along the cathedral's axis. Of course, this rule was just a general principle. It was not always adhered to. The founders of such buildings were nothing if not pragmatic people, with an understanding that occasionally one must work under special conditions in which the rules do not work properly and so they must be modified. It is the skill of the master that allows him or her to know just when the rules do not apply. Special conditions may sometimes have overridden the ideal, and so other orientations can be found occasionally. But even when they are aberrant, they are still related to the overall geometrical pattern of the building.

In the period when these buildings were erected, there were two common systems of sacred geometry in use. The older appears to be that known as *ad quadratum*, which is based upon the square and its derivatives. It is related directly to the fourfold structure of the human body, and the eightfold division of space and time. Thus, it is the symbolic epitome of order, stability and continuity. The younger, and in some respects a more dynamic system, is from the equilateral triangle, *ad triangulum*. *Ad quadratum* is formed directly from the square and the octagram, the overlapping of two squares to make a regular eight-pointed figure. The initial square, orientated in the manner approved by the locator and masons in charge of the work, was overlain by a second square of the same size. This, at an angle of 45° to the first square, formed the starting-point of ad quadratum geometry. According to medieval tradition, this form was developed by a master mason of

Fig. 43. Certain French occultists have claimed that this seven-pointed Hermetic Star of the Templars lies across France, linking certain places of power once connected with the Knights Templar. Each of them corresponds with a specific planetary virtue.

Strasbourg, Albertus Argentinus. In later German masonic writings, this figure is called *acht-uhr*, or *acht-ort*, 'eight-hour' or 'eight-place'. This name alludes to the traditional eightfold division of the horizon, the day, the year, weights and measures that are inherent in the European spiritual tradition.

From this initial octagram, the whole geometry of a church could be developed, in one of two ways. The first method, the true *acht-ort*, developed a series of octagrams, inside and outside. These were drawn directly from the first figure. This system can be seen, *inter alia*, at the cathedrals of Ely in England, Verdun in France and Bamberg in Germany. Basically, this is the technique used in Romanesque buildings. However, by the late medieval period, the system of *ad quadratum* had become refined further into a more complex system, based upon the double rather than the single square. This form, it will be remembered, was favoured since Egyptian antiquity as a shape fitting for a sacred enclosure.

The second and later version of *ad quadratum* produced the elegantly-proportioned geometrical complex known as the *dodecaïd*, a twelve-pointed irregular polygon which lent itself admirably to church planning. Like the simple *acht-ort* of the earlier *ad quadratum*, the basic figure was an octagram. However, the first square from which the octagram was derived was itself extended to form a double square. From this second square, another octagram was constructed. This made a figure composed of two contiguous squares with overlapping squares set at 45° to the initial double square. Upon this interlaced octagram, a larger square was superimposed. This was defined by the places at which it cut the inner intersections of the two octagrams.

The *dodecaïd* is a richly symbolic figure. The three overlapping squares have at their centre a small square that is common to all three. According to Trinitarian Christian symbolism, this central square is taken to represent the essential unity of the triune godhead. The central square is larger than the others, symbolising the Father god of the Christian trinity. The frame of the double square which pervades the Trinity, embodies the four elements and also the four cardinal directions, symbolising the material world interpenetrated and sustained by the Divine Power. The whole is a synopsis of the numbers three and four, the mystic seven.

When the *dodecaïd* is applied to the fabric of an actual church, the four corners of the double square mark the four foundations of the church, the cornerstones upon which the actual building is supported. The easternmost of the three 45°-orientated squares represents the Son. Its centre is the focus upon which the altar ought to stand, where, each day, through the celebration of the Mass, Christians believe Christ is present in the form of the Host and the wine. The central and larger square, that of the Father, is centred at the church's *omphalos*, the heart of the building. To the west of this is the square that symbolises the Holy Spirit. At the *locus,* the font should stand, the place where the Holy Spirit is conjured into the neophyte at her or his baptism. The centre-points of the Son and the spirit reflect the esoteric layout of the Tabernacle of the Israelites where the Ark of the Covenant and the altar occupied comparable positions.

The essence of divine architecture is very simple. Ideally, all parts of the sacred ensemble from the paraphernalia and vestments of the clergy to the form and structure of the whole sacred enclosure is be derived from one symbolic harmonic system figure. If this is carried out according to proper principles, all of the dimensions, locations and relationships within the sacred place will be related directly to this system. Inn so being, they are integrated with the whole of creation. They are not an arbitrary imposition on the natural world by unthinking humans, but a genuine outgrowth of Nature.

IDEA GEOMETRICAE ARCHITECTONICAE AB ICHNOGRAPHIA SVMPTA. VT PERAMVSSINEAS POSSINT
PER ORTHOGRAPHIAM AC SCAENOGRAPHIAM PERDVCERE OMNES QVASCVNQVAE LINEAS. NON
SOLVM AD CIRCINI CENTRVM. SED QVAE A TRIGONO ET QVADRATO AVT ALIO QVOVISMODO
PERVENIVNT POSSINT SVVM HABERE RESPONSVM. TVM PER EVRYTHMIAM, PROPOR-
TIONATAM QVANTVM ETIAMB SYMMETRIAE QVANTITATEM; ORDINARIAM AC PER
OPERIS·DECORATIONEM OSTENDERE. VTI ETIAM HEC QVAE A GERMANICO MORE PERVE
NIVNT DISTRIBVENTVR BENE QVEMADMODVM SACRA CATHEDRALIS AEDES MEDIOLANI
PATET. ELO· 4 . .P. M. G. A. A. P. VL: Q2. C. AC. AF. D .

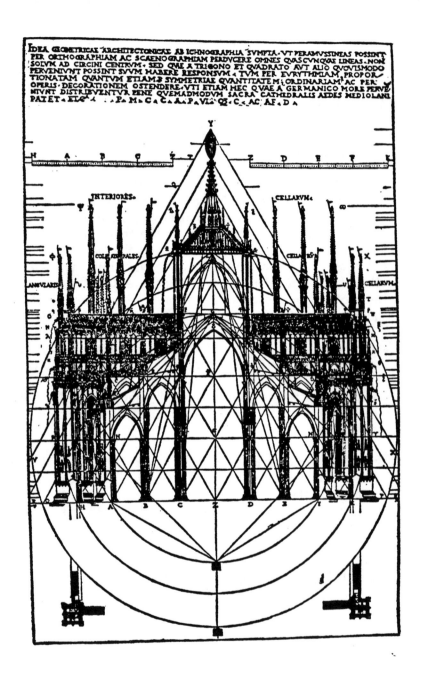

144

Chapter 18

The Parameteric Method

In 1992, one of the great secrets of the European esoteric tradition was made public by Joy Hancox in her remarkable book *The Byrom Collection*, in which she explores the esoteric spiritual background of an exceptional English polymath of the eighteenth century, John Byrom. During her researches, Joy Hancox asked me my opinion of some of the remarkable esoteric diagrams which Byrom had owned. At once I recognised that they were more than just an incomprehensible collection of circles and lines, but were indeed the symbolic encoding of architectural proportional geometry in parameteric diagrams. Parameteric diagrams (incidentally wrongly edited as *parametric* in the appendix of Hancox's *The Byrom Collection*, where I comment on them) are drawings that contain the parameters for a building. This way of describing structure is quite different from a plan, for parameteric diagrams are the encoding of dimensions and geometric ratios in graphic form. Usually, they look like a series of concentric circles, completely incomprehensible to anyone not privy to the inner traditions of the locators.

Fig. 44. The guiding geometry of the great medieval cathedral at Milano in Italy was recorded in this engraving from Caesare Caesariano's edition of *The Ten Books on Architecture* by Vitruvius, which was published in 1521. The underlying patterns are a simplified version of the parameteric diagrams preserved in the Byrom Collection.

Byrom's drawings are composed of a series of concentric circles at irregular intervals, with additional dots and lines. Emerging from the main body of these concentric is a linear component. The divisions of this part are related directly to those of the main body, extending beyond the circles themselves. Such parameteric diagrams were the means of recording and transmitting the key dimensions and proportions of a certain building,

The diagrams preserved by Byrom contain the specific proportions of certain London theatres of Shakespeare's day, including The Globe and The Swan. In their form, parameteric diagrams resemble some published drawings from the tradition of operative freemasonry, such as Caesare Caesariano's diagram of Milano Cathedral, published in his 1521 edition of Vitruvius's *The Ten Books on Architecture*. Although it shows the actual plan of the cathedral, which parameteric diagrams do not, Caeseriano's diagram shows the cathedral's plan and elevation projected upon a series of concentric circles. Caesariano's engraving is more explicit than these parameteric diagrams, for it shows the actual ground plan and elevation of the cathedral, superimposed upon the lines that define their dimensions.

The parameteric means of encoding and transmitting geometrical and proportional information is elegantly economical: the dimensions and proportions for an entire building are set forth in a single diagram, from which all of the necessary dimensions, proportions and related geometrical forms of the construction can be readily determined. Because of this, they were inscribed as lines on the solar gilded balls that support the cross or weathercock on many churches in mainland Europe.

In the Rhineland, it is said that these balls contain the plan of the church, so that, if it is burnt down, another can be made the same as the old one. The balls are invariably empty, for they do not contain plans on paper or lead sheet, but themselves are three-dimensional parameteric structures that encode the entire harmonic system of the church over which they stand.

Unlike modern plans and elevations, parameteric diagrams express an almost hidden aspect of the European traditional way of looking at the world. This traditional mode of thought and perception differs radically from the modern approach, for it is holistic. On the contrary,the modern way of thinking is largely fragmental. Things are 'deconstructed', taken apart in a reductionist way, and then examined in isolation. Only when each 'part' has been examined is the whole considered. Unfortunately, this way of looking at the world produces a false view of it, where the observed is lulled into the perception that the operating, real, whole is actually composed of an assemblage of those parts which have been put together in the manner of manufacturing.

Modern technical drawings that consist of plan and elevation, details, sectioning, etc. are examples of this fragmental view of existence. They are based upon a conception of cubic geometry that divides space into three dimensions at right angles to one another, the axes X, Y and Z. Then, every component of the machine or building is described in terms of these three axes. It is an admirably workable way of designing and describing components to be manufactured, but it is all too easy to consider it to be the 'correct' way of presenting all information. As the dominant means to-day, we should always be aware that it is merely one of the several possibilities. Parameteric diagrams are another.

Parameteric diagrams are pre-industrial in origin. They are the product of a more traditional, alternative possibility of symbolic presentation, a holistic understanding where the traditional proportional system of the building or structure is not divided artificially into elevation and plan, but serves as the inherent rule for all of the parts, whatever they are and wherever they may be located. The parameteric approach enabled the master carpenter and master mason to incorporate the classical virtues of order, eurhythmy and symmetry into their buildings. A correct application of proportional and harmonic parameters into the original diagram will invariably result in the presence of these qualities and virtues in the final building. In the present day, the use of parameteric diagrams could be reintroduced with advantage in the design of new buildings. This is part of the program of the Honourable Guild of Locators. The re-emergence of parameteric methods at this time has been an important contribution to a new understanding of the vast potential that the Western Tradition of architecture still holds.

Chapter 19

The Symbols of Process

Alchemy is a philosophy of Nature that symbolically links the cosmos with the human being. In the Islamic tradition, which preserved and shaped alchemy during the persecution of scientific thought by the Christian churches, it is considered to be *sina'ah*, simultaneously an art and a science, that which according to English culture is a true craft. In its purely material aspect, alchemy can be seen as ancestral to modern chemistry. But it also has another, deeper, more significant, aspect, the psychic. In this aspect, alchemy can be seen as a sophisticated form of spiritual psychology. Like the other spiritual crafts, alchemy has as its basis the concept expressed in the Old English motto *In on is al* - in one is all. Everything in existence partakes of the quality of everything else, in that all things that we recognise as individual separate entities can be viewed as being merely aspects of the whole, as in the Hermetic Maxim. For example, "Our spirits are our bodies, and our bodies our spirits" was the maxim of the Fifth and Sixth Shi'ite Imams in whose milieu alchemy was developed into something resembling its classical form.

The task of the alchemist is to conduct the process that leads to the transmutation of the substance of existence through the agency of a spiritual power represented by the Philosophers' Stone. This is certainly not a natural process, for it cannot take place without human agency. Ultimately, the function of alchemy is to assist evolution, using technology in the service of spirit to bring higher principles into the physical plane,

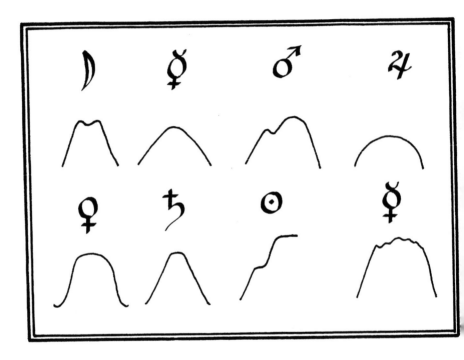

resulting in the perfection of Nature. Alchemy operates on two levels simultaneously: on the material level, it is an attempt to refine and perfect matter by altering the subtle balances within it; whilst on the human level it is the process of bringing about an inner transformation that leads to the perfection of the individual. Both functions are symbolic and spiritual, which separates alchemy from the physical sciences with which it is sometimes compared. But as early as 1786, Dom Pernety, in his *Greek and Egyptian Fables Revealed* recognised that: "Vulgar chemistry is the art of destroying compounds formed by Nature, whilst the alchemy of the Hermeticists is the art of working with Nature to perfect them". In this, Pernety was following the scientists of ancient Alexandria, who saw alchemists as spiritual midwives who delivered gold from the womb of Nature.

The invention of alchemy is credited traditionally to Hermes Trismegistos in ancient Egypt. But it was in Alexandria that technicians developed the craft. Alexandria was unique in the ancient west because it contained a publicly-funded centre of academic excellence that was not subservient to the interests of business tycoons or military magnates, but to the pursuit of knowledge as a means for the development and perfection of the individual. The Museum of Alexandria, dedicated to the nine Muses, was the greatest university of the classical world, with the most comprehensive library ever assembled in that age. In the pluralistic Alexandrian milieu, spiritual technicians from several ethnic backgrounds, most notably Ostanes, Agathodaimon, Bolos Democritos, Teukros, Jamasb al-Hakim and Maria the Jewess played an important part in developing the science. Their works, along with other material, made up the corpus of alchemical literature known as the *Corpus*

Fig. 45. The geomantic correspondences of hill and mountain shapes to the planets, according to the European tradition of *location*. As above, so below.

Hermeticum, named after the founder and spiritual support of the craft, Hermes Trismegistos.

When the Arabs invaded Egypt, the city of Alexandria was sold out by the Byzantine Emperor. Although his army in Egypt was larger than the Islamic forces, and at a strategic advantage, nevertheless he shamefully negotiated with the Arabs for a ceasefire of several months during which he withdrew all of his troops from the city by sea. Those citizens who had sufficient money to escape also fled to more secure parts of the Empire, before the Islamic army entered the demoralised city without a fight. The parallel with the abandonment of Hong Kong to the Chinese Communists by the British Government in our day is striking. Thus the alchemical texts and techniques left behind in Alexandria were part of the booty that the Arabs took for themselves. Alchemy passed into the realm of Islam, and soon Hermes Trismegistos was absorbed into Islamic mythology as part of the 'golden chain of prophecy' that began with Adam and ended with Mohammed. All of the arts of Hermes, including alchemy and divinatory geomancy, were thus absorbed into Islamic orthodoxy, preserved and developed.

The Ummayyad Prince Khalid ibn Yazid is considered to be the first Islamic alchemist in the Alexandrian tradition. He learned the craft from Morienus, an Alexandrian Christian, who himself had been an apprentice of the celebrated alchemist Zosimus. However, Jabir ibn Hayyan (c.712 - c. 815), the court alchemist of Harun al-Rashid of Baghdad, is the key historical figure in the development of alchemy, known in the west as Geber. Credited with inventing, among other scientific apparatus, the capillary syphon, he is associated with developing further the classical theory of the four elements (fire, air, water and earth), by introducing the concepts of the four qualities or virtues of matter. These are the qualities dry and moist, hot and cold. His system of classification teaches that the elements come into being when substance is combined with a pair of these virtues. Thus, the element of fire is composed of dry heat and substance; air, of moist heat with substance; water, of moist cold substance; and earth of dry coldness with substance. Like all occult scientists of note, Jabir ibn Hayyan was a polymath who recognised no artificial boundaries between spiritual knowledge, mathematics and a detailed investigation of the properties of the natural world.

Although he was a devout Sufi, Jabir ibn Hayyan accepted and followed the ancient Pagan symbolic philosophy that teaches that the earth is alive. According to this viewpoint, matter is not inert, but part of an organism that lives and grows. Jabir ibn Hayyan taught that metals grow in the earth from different combinations of Mercury and Sulphur according to planetary influences. The Mercury and Sulphur of alchemy are not just the physical elements of modern chemistry, but, like the planets, symbolic descriptions of qualities whose virtues are present most perfectly in Mercury and Sulphur.

The connection of metals with the heavens is of course more ancient than the days of Jabir ibn Hayyan, being part of the inner teachings of the *Philosophia Perennis*. In the traditions of European location, for instance, the different shapes of mountains are classified according to their planetary rulers, as are certain corresponding parts of the human body. The alchemical sigils that stand for the metals are the same as for their corresponding planets. Saturn shares its sigil with Lead, its 'insignia' on the terrestrial plane. Likewise, the sigil for the planet (or planetary deity) called Jupiter is that of its corresponding metal, Tin. Mars shares its sigil with the martial metal Iron, whilst the bright golden Sun corresponds with Gold. Venus corresponds with Copper, whilst the name Mercury is used both for the planet and the metal, whose alternative name, Quicksilver, is now considered archaic. Finally, the silvery Moon corresponds with Silver.

According to Jabirean alchemy, each metal has an inner and an outer aspect. Two of its qualities are inner and two outer, so that, for instance, outwardly, Gold is hot and humid, whilst inwardly it is cold and dry. Silver, its complementary opposite is

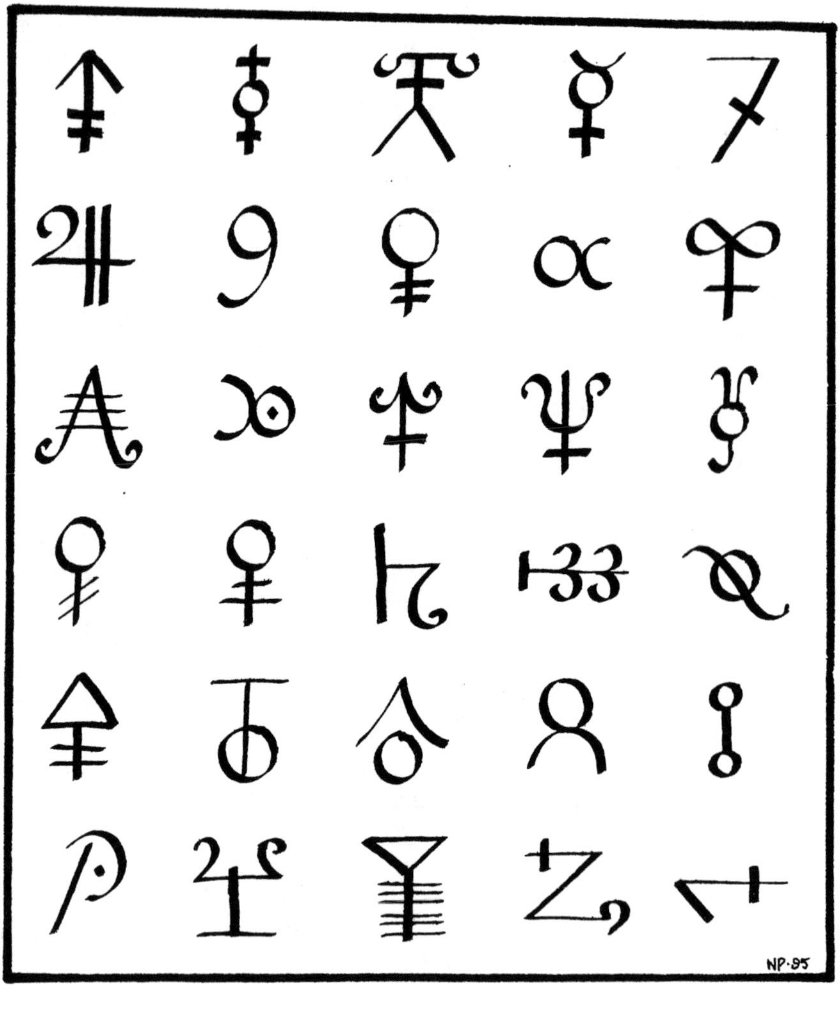
NP·95

outwardly a combination of cold and dry whilst inwardly it is hot and humid. Each metal is thus some combination of the fourfold virtues of matter. In Jabir's alchemy, the inner nature of materials depends upon *al-mizan*, their balance. This balance describes the relative qualities and virtues that determine the esoteric nature of any alchemical substance. It can be described but not defined, and thus it exists on the symbolic level, where it is expressed not in contemporary scientific terminology, but in terms of numerology, geometrical figures, alphabet-symbolism and sigils, comparable with the ramifications of runic symbology in northern Europe.

This balance is symbolised by the alchemical serpent, The Worm Oroboros, conventionally depicted as a snake or Nwyvre biting its own tail. The Coptic alchemical papyrus known as *Kleopatra Chrysopoeia (The Gold-Making of Cleopatra)*, dating from the third century and preserved at Leiden in the Netherlands, shows the most celebrated image of Oroboros, with the Greek words "One is All" within. Balance can be defined numerically, and, according to Jabirean alchemy, the four virtues are present in each metal in a fixed ratio, that is 1:3:5:8. As is to be expected in traditional sciences, this numerical sequence is significant also in Babylonian sacred architecture and Pythagorean musical theory. It is related directly to the canonical harmonic systems that were used by the masters of the Western Tradition in building classical temples, churches, synagogues, mosques and masonic lodges.

Fig. 46. Alchemical sigils of metals, minerals and other materials. These are but a few of a whole system of noation that has a sigil for each and every element, mineral, metal and material in existence. Top line: 1. Iron; 2. Haematite; 3. Lead; 4. Mercury; 5. Tin. Second line: 1. Steel; 2. Silver; 3. Copper; 4. Gold; 5. Glass. Line three: 1. Amalgam; 2. Platinum; 3. Arsenic; 4. Antimony; 5. Natural Sulphur. Fourth line: 1. Bell matal; 2. Brass; 3. Lapis lazuli; 4. Cinnabar; 5. Bronze. Fifth line: 1. Phosphorus; 2. Manganese; 3. Zinc; 4. Cobalt; 5. Nickel. Sixth line: 1. Bismuth; 2. Alum; 3. Talc; 4: Lime; 5. Wax.

To define the balance, Jabir subdivides each quality into four *degrees*, which are further subdivided into seven *minutes*. Each of the 28 *minutes* corresponds with one of the letters of the Arabic alphabet. The name of the metal in Arabic is thus related to the corresponding balances of subtle qualities that compose the metal. According to the Hermetic viewpoint, metals like lead and iron are seen as imperfect reflections of the true, perfected metal, gold. By adjusting the balances through complex physical processes, it is possible, claim the alchemists, to transmute baser metals into gold. Similarly, by using the correct harmonic principles in architecture or indeed the manufacture of any artifacts, it is possible to bring them into a state of perfection as reflections of Paradise.

From Islamic sources, through Islamic Spain and also the Crusades, alchemical knowledge passed into the mainstream European mystical current. In the 12th century, a portion of Jabir ibn Hayyan's considerable works was translated into Latin by Gerard of Cremona, whose own works on divinatory geomancy were influential in Europe (for further details of this, see my book, The *Oracle of Geomancy*, Capall Bann, 1995). The classification of Nature into the three kingdoms of mineral, vegetable and animal, devised by the alchemist Muhammad ibn Zakariyya al-Razi, entered European tradition at this time. Such developments demonstrate that the spiritual arts are not fundamentalistic, but have developed and evolved continuously over the centuries. However, this has led sometimes to a denaturing of the spiritual content and the emergence of something new and unprecedented. Al-Razi is the perfect example of this, for, although he was an alchemist, through his philosophical approach to matter, rejecting the symbolic view of Nature in favour of a literalistic one, he was the founder of the science of chemistry, which has led both to great benefits and great destructiveness.

Although alchemy is often portrayed by historians of science as a primitive forerunner of scientific chemistry, this is not the whole story. It is certainly true that modern chemistry emerged from alchemy through the work of al-Razi, as much as it did from traditional pharmacy and metalworking. But scientific chemistry does not have anything to say about the symbolic world, and consequently this, the most significant element of alchemy, is downgraded in importance by historians. Alchemy is a system of symbols, yet it is not a formula, which, if followed religiously, will lead invariably to the same result. In this, it differs from the scientific method. The Great Work that results in the alchemist's creation of the Great Red Elixir or Philosopher's Stone is a symbol of inner freedom.

The Great Red Elixir and the Philosopher's Stone appear throughout the alchemical history of Europe. For instance, the Parisian alchemical husband-and-wife partnership of Nicolas and Perrenelle Flamel is claimed to have created the Great Red Elixir, and through it, to have transmuted base metals into Gold. Like all technicians, both spiritual and profane, Nicolas Flamel (1330 - 1418) asserted that by its all-inclusive nature, his craft, that is, alchemy, transcends both religion and morality. The researches that he conducted in collaboration with his wife, Perrenelle, were based on the work of Abraham the Jew, whose book he acquired in 1357. Unable to work the operations described in the book, the Flamels visited Santiago de Compostela in Spain, where they met a Jewish wise man who had, so he said, converted to Catholicism. Nevertheless, he was an expert on the Qabalah. Having gained useful knowledge from the Jewish sage, it is said that Nicolas and Perrenelle made three successful transmutations using the Red Elixir to convert Mercury into wonderfully ductile soft Gold.

Because Islamic law prohibits images, alchemical symbolism in the Muslim world was restricted to numerology, arithromancy, gematria and notarikon. In Europe, however, this was not the case, and emblematical symbolic illustrations became the means for transmitting alchemical knowledge as they were before the fall of Alexandria. The enigmatic *Book of Abraham the Jew*, from which the Flamels derived their technique, is said to have contained mainly symbolic drawings. Later

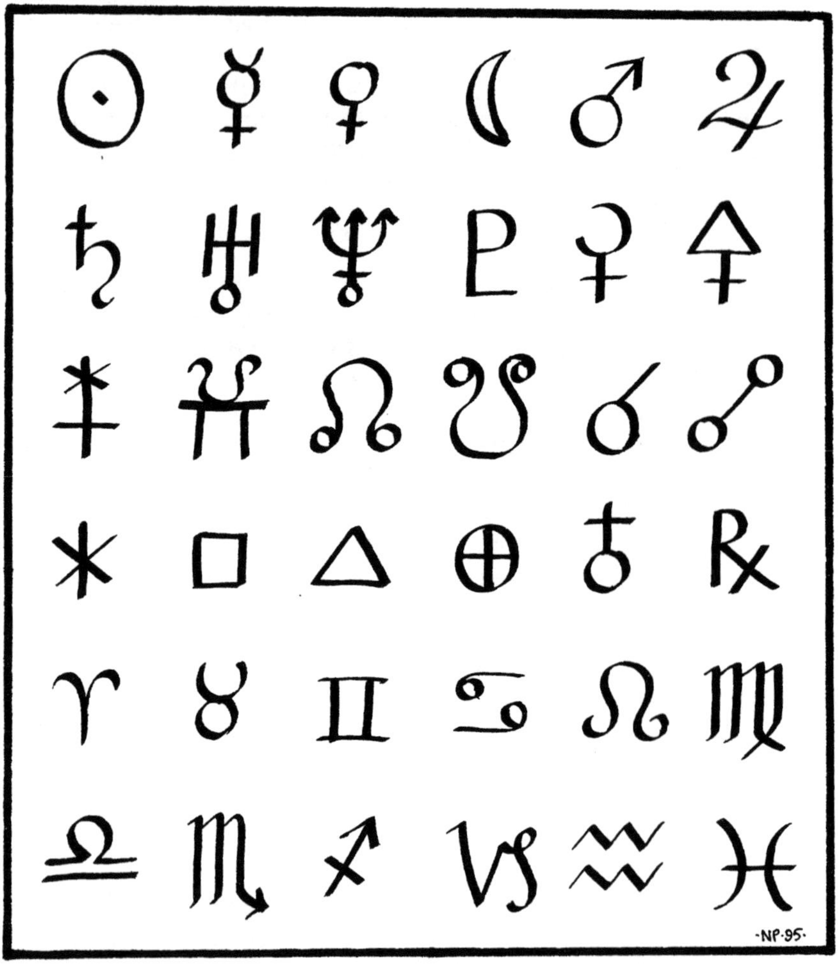
·NP·95·

alchemical works are certainly filled with wonderful symbolic engravings that in the 20th century attracted C. G. Jung to analyse them according to his psychological theories. For example Flamel's book, *Le Livre des figures hieroglyphiques* (The Book of Hieroglyphic Figures) refer to the emblematical paintings that he made in the Cemetery of the Innocents in Paris after alchemy was made illegal by King Charles V, and he was forced, at least in public, to give up the craft. Many later printed alchemical texts by authors such as Michael Maier, Johannes Mylius, Basilius Valentinus, Pierre Savouret, Lambsprink and others are among the most significant European artworks of their era.

The career of the alchemist in medieval Europe was not at all easy. Occasional persecutions by churchmen who suspected practitioners of heresy, and kings who feared the undermining of the economic system by gold manufacture, ended the lives of several alchemists. The English alchemist Thomas Daulton,was reported to king Edward IV as having made the Philosopher's Stone, and then was hounded to produce Gold for the king. After escaping, Daulton was imprisoned and executed.

Thomas Norton, who lived in the fifteenth century, demonstrates the kind of world in which the occult scientist is

---

Fig. 47. Alchemical and astrological sigils of planets, etc.: Line one: 1. The Sun; 2. Mercury; 3. Venus; 4. The Moon; 5. Mars; 6. Jupiter. Line two: 1. Saturn; 2. Uranus; 3. Neptune; 4. Pluto; 5. Ceres; 6. Pallas. Third line: 1. Juno; 2. Vesta; 3. Caput Draconis, the ascending node of the Moon and corresponding figure in divinatory geomancy; 4. Cauda Draconis, descending node of the Moon and geomantic figure; 5. Conjunction (astrological); 6. Opposition (180 degrees). Line four: 1. Sextile (60 degrees); 2. Square (90 degrees); 3. Trine (120 degrees); 4. The Earth; 5. Alternative sigil for the Earth, or alchemical Antimony; 6. Retrograde. Line five: 1. Aries; 2. Taurus; 3. Gemini; 4. Cancer; 5. Leo; 6. Virgo. Line six: 1. Libra; 2. Scorpio; 3. Sagittarius; 4. Capricorn; 5. Aquarius; 6. Pisces.

forced to live, as well as the link between alchemy and sacred architecture. At the age of 28, Norton, who was a disciple of the alchemist-priest George Ripley, Canon of Bridlington, made the Great Red Elixir. Unfortunately, it was stolen by a servant, and disappeared. Undeterred by this setback, Norton undertook the lengthy alchemical process for a second time, and was successful once more. But he had not learnt from his previous experiences. He lost it to the wife of the master mason, William Canynges, who used it in the design and building of the remarkable church of St Mary Redcliffe in Bristol. It is famed to this day for its stunning sixfold *ad triangulum* geometry and the unique labyrinth roof boss.

Norton later wrote a book that attempted to transmit alchemical knowledge that hitherto had been kept among the secrets revealed only orally to initiates. This was published much later by Elias Ashmole (1617 - 1692) in his *Theatrum Chimicum Britannicum*. Written in 1477, Thomas Norton's work was created at the same time that the geometrical secrets of the operative freemasons were being revealed to non-initiates (for details of this, see the author's *Sacrad Geometry*, Capall Bann, 1995).

Chapter 20

Alchemy: The Revealed Tradition

European alchemical symbolism is presented as a fourfold process, which the operative alchemist undertakes in his or her laboratory work. One of the most explicit versions of this process is presented in Salomon Trismosin's work, *Splendor Solis (The Sun's Splendour)*. As an old man, Trismosin, according to works attributed to him, claimed to have prepared the Philosopher's Stone, with which he was rejuvenated, and lived over 150 years. After beginning with a plate showing two philosophers before the Temple of Alchemy, which is ruled by the Sun and Moon, *Splendor Solis* depicts an alchemist pointing at an alembic vessel, saying, "Let us go to seek the nature of the four elements". Then, the work is commenced by the activation of the double fountain of Mercury, where the adept is exhorted to make one water from two waters. "You, who seek to create the Sun and Moon", we are told, "give them to drink of the Inimical Wine".

The next plate of *Splendor Solis* depicts the Sun and Moon, in whose union all opposites may be brought together. This is the opening of the vessel, the first conjunction of the alchemist's work. Next, the alchemist must penetrate into the inner parts of the earth, entering by way of a cave in a mountainside. There, having descended into the depths of Annwn, he encounters the shades of Ahasuerus, Bigthan, Esther, Mordecai and Teresh. Next, having shamanically travelled down into the underworld, the alchemist ascends the cosmic axis of the Hermetic Tree by means of a ladder, to the upperworld where he can pick the fruit. As he climbs, numerous birds, the symbol of spirit, fly into the air from the tree. Beneath, naked women bathe in a bath that recalls the spring of the Norns at the foot of Yggdrassil.

The seventh plate of *Splendor Solis* depicts an old king drowning in the sea, to be superseded by his son, who bears a sceptre whose apex is crowned with the seven planetary lights. Here, through the death of the old we encounter the development of the star of perfection of the seven planets, which is empowered by the beams of light radiating from a star whose splendour almost matches that of the Sun with which it is twinned in the sky. Through the death and putrefaction of the drowned king, we reach the stage of Nigredo, or blackening, portrayed in the eighth plate by a black man rising from the mire to greet the angelically-winged white queen. She clothes the black man in a purple robe and raises him up to the bright light, and takes him with her to heaven, according to the accompanying text.

By this process, the black man is transformed to white, symbolising the alchemical stage known as Albedo, the whitening, work of cleansing. In operative alchemy, this involves the reflux distillation of the elements and their calcination in the 'fire of reverberation'. This produces the fusion of the whitened black man and the angelic queen into a two-headed hermaphrodite, which represents the second, White Conjunction. This *Splendor Solis* figure depicts the hermaphrodite holding a target in his/her right hand and an egg in the left. The egg represents the fermentation of the white stone, symbol of the Philosopher's Stone, whilst the circular target bears concentric rings that represent the four elements and the four stages of existence of Druidic cosmology.

The tenth plate in *Splendor Solis* depicts the aftermath of the second conjunction, which is the slaying and dismembering of the body. This signifies the alchemical stage of Citrinitas, yellow death and putrefaction. Then the body is boiled in a cauldron in which it is again regenerated, and the spirit returned to it in the shape of a spirit-bird in the form of a white dove. This is the third, Yellow Conjunction.

The twelfth figure of *Splendor Solis* depicts an alchemical vessel under the rulership of the planet Mercury in which a boy encounters a nwyvre, and pours fluid into its mouth. The accompanying text tells us "A wondrous light will be seen in the darkness". The next six *Splendor Solis* figures also show crowned alchemical vessels containing various emblematic and symbolic entities and beasts. Like the first vessel, they are each under the rulership of one of the planets. Under Jupiter, whose chariot is depicted as being pulled by Peacocks - Juno's bird, a black and white doves tumble together as if in combat. The next vessel, under the rulership of Mars, whose chariot is drawn by foxes, contains a three-headed bird, with the text "The heat cleanses that which is unclean". The triadic bird represents the purification process in which the useless impurities are removed, and the essential Elixir is produced. Around the vessel, war rages. This is the accomplishment of the fourth and final alchemical stage known as Rubedo, red death and putrefaction.

The fourth crowned vessel that brings us towards the completion of the Great Work is ruled by Saturn, whose chariot is pulled by two black horses. Inside, the three-headed bird is transformed now into a three-headed dragon, rearing up ready to fight. This is the 'hidden thing' of the philosophers. The person who can find such a 'hidden thing' "is a master of the art". Next, beneath the rulership of Venus, riding in her bird-hauled car, a splendid peacock fills the vessel. The multi-coloured peacock's tail (*Cauda Pavonis*) signifies the return of the soul to the matter in question. The next plate, ruled by the Sun in his cockerel-drawn car, depicts the queen. Surrounding her, men pursue the seven liberal arts of traditional learning. The eighteenth plate of *Splendor Solis* is ruled by the Moon.

XVI

THE TOWER.

Inside the alchemical vessel is the solar king,, whilst around him, men hunt and fish. Here, the fire is at its end, not burning hot, but under the rule of air, and therefore in a stable state, approaching the end. Plates 17 and 18 thus depict the fourth, Red Conjunction of Sun and Moon.

The final four plates of *Splendor Solis* show the lunar body conjoining with the golden ferment, or Solar Sulphur. This is followed by a plate of mothers watching and helping their children at play, who denote the final coagulation of the matter that builds towards the final accomplishment of the Great Work. The next place shows nine washerwomen at work, washing and drying linen, symbolising the renewal of the fabric of the world that is the aim of the alchemist. Washerwomen represent continuity, the necessary maintenance of the present that is personified by the middle Fate, Clotho, or the Norn Verdandi, 'that which is becoming'. Alchemically, the nine washerwomen signify the final sublimation of the earthly elements into "the spirit of the quintessence, known as the tincture. *fermentum, anima* or oil, which is the very next matter to the Stone of the Philosophers". The final, twenty-second plate of *Splendor Solis* (corresponding with the 22 letters of the Hebrew alphabet) is the Splendour of the Sun itself, when the solar stone or Red Elixir is produced, putting together all natural things, "so that there may be a unified structure". Thus is the Great Work accomplished.

But this is not the end of the story. Nothing on earth is static, and if anything is to have continuance and not to disappear,

---

Fig. 48. The Tarot major arcanum XVI, The Tower, from Nigel Pennick's *Way of the Eight Winds Tarot*, is the image of what happens when human beings attempt to go too far with Nature. In recent times, this mistake, exemplified by the Biblical tale of the Tower of Babel, has been made manifest in the nuclear power station disasters at Windscale in England (1957) and Chernobyl in the Ukraine (1986).

then it must retain some value. In the middle of the twentieth century, the Swiss psychologist C.G. Jung showed convincingly that the symbolism of the stages of alchemy could be related to the hidden structure and processes of the human psyche. Also, the further reaches of operative alchemy impinge in weird ways upon contemporary chemical science. Basilius Valentinus, the Benedictine monk-alchemist from Erfurt in Thuringia, Germany, used Antimony along with Mercury in his alchemical work, seeking the Elixir. The modern controversy over the alleged existence of Red Mercury, a uniquely powerful chemical explosive, echoes his experiments in the 1400s. Like the Great Red Elixir, even the existence of Red Mercury is hotly disputed. If it can be made, it would be a compound of pure Mercury and Mercury Antimony Oxide that is said to be cherry red in colour and semi-liquid in consistency. According to reports, theoretically Red Mercury is an explosive material that could release, weight for weight, thousands of times more chemical energy than TNT.

Some scientists fear that Red Mercury may have applications in fusion weapons that, like other nuclear weapons, are the inversion of alchemy made real. Contemporary alchemists consider that the transmutation of elements in nuclear reactors achieves in physical reality the exact opposite of the aim of alchemy. Instead of perfecting matter in a spiritual way, it subverts the evolution of the mineral kingdom, bringing irresistible destruction in its wake. The aim of the ancient alchemists, whether Pagan, Jewish, Muslim or Christian, was certainly the opposite of the devastation wrought at Hiroshima, Nagasaki, Windscale, Three Mile Island and Chernobyl. But still it cannot be denied that nuclear technology is a direct outgrowth of a process that started with the operative alchemy of the Somerset Franciscan monk, Roger Bacon (1214 - 1292), who, in addition to being considered one of the founders of the experimental method, also invented gunpowder, with results that are well known.

Chapter 21

Writing: The Cosmos Analysed

To describe the ever-flowing state of existence, the ancient Bardic teachings of Britain speak of *Manred*, by which they mean the underlying matrix of matter. In contemporary fragmental terminology, *Manred* is the atoms, molecules and geometrical relationships that are the fabric of physical reality. *Manred* is impossible to describe in words, for, unlike language, which is linear, Manred comprises itself seamlessly, and hence is non-linear. The best means of appreciating *Manred* is to watch the ever-flowing patterns of swirling water in a fast-flowing brook, though even this is a mere fragment of the whole. The work of the ancient Celtic artisans displays the ever-changing patterns of *Manred* in artistic form.

The geometric matrices upon which Celtic tesselations, spirals and knotwork are based are continuous. In their plurality, tesselations, spirals and knotwork are interchangeable. They fade into one another. These patterns are fixed artistic representations of the ever-flowing particles of *Manred*, for all is flux, and the patterns we see at any one time are the patterns of that time, not eternal and unchanging. It is the essence of *Manred* in tangible form that is the Red Elixir. As the perceptive German architect Hans Poelzig once pointed out, "Form arises out of the mystic abyss".

Alphabets, like language, are a metaphysical means of describing reality, enabling those that employ them to experience transformative processes. Writing is a means of

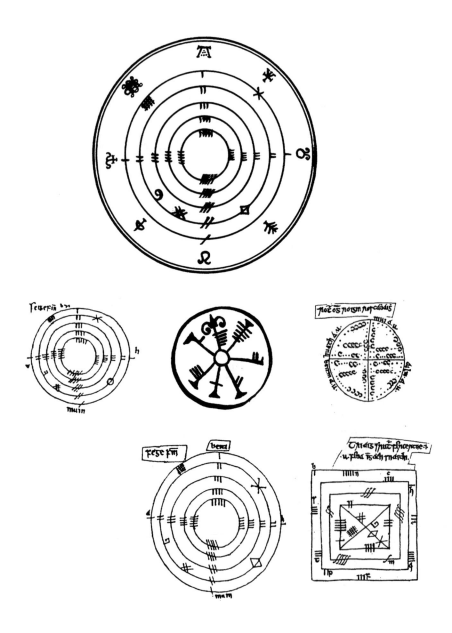

providing conscious images of a reality that cannot be comprehended by any other means. It is used to go beyond the outward appearance of things, to express human concepts that have no being in the physical cosmos. Through the exercise of the human faculty of consciousness, we can explore deeper meanings that we perceive within reality. Operating in the present in a dynamic way, the human consciousness, flowing like *Manred* and never static, undertakes a continuous process of recombination, ever newly creating new experiences that provide insights, express concepts, describe structures, feelings, and the otherwise-inexplicable nature of transvolution.

When used esoterically, certain aspects of alphabets can convey meaning that cannot be expressed adequately by any other means. Then, the become true symbols that can express non-verbal experiences that can have a noticeable effect on human awareness. Used properly, they can change suddenly the direction of flow of one's mind, diverting it into new and unexpected channels. Users of magical alphabets especially are enabled to experience a flood of new understanding, accompanied by an immediate recognition of completely new viewpoints of life. After one has undergone such an experience, every aspect of life is transformed. The accomplishment of such an inner transformation is the main objective of the magical use of alphabets.

Considered beyond their strictly utilitarian function, alphabets represent the presence of the infinite within the finite. What exactly is the infinite is another matter, which may be

---

Fig. 49. Fionn's Wheel or Fionn's Shield are the alternative names for the series of Irish diagrams that encompass the Cetic tree alphabet of Ogham. Like the runic wheels, the wheels and shields of Fionn MacCumhaill relate the wattles and the branches to the directions and time, creating a magical sigil of great power to equal the Germanic Aegishjalmur.

expressed according to any number of internally-consistent philosophical systems. To the theist, this intangible quality may be viewed as the means by which the creator is present within the world, whilst, on a less dogmatic level, it signifies the many as-yet unrealized possibilities of existence that can come into being should the right conditions become manifest. The individual characters that comprise any alphabet can be viewed as metaphors of reality. In themselves, the vast majority of individual characters or sigils have no transcendent external meaning: whatever meaning they possess is in the minds of the people who use them or have learnt them. The only transcendent forms are those which are examples of the various geometrical forms which can be perceived in natural structures. In principle, individual alphabet characters are complex symbolic structures that operate only within the context of the specific alphabet to which they are attached. This is apparent because the same shape-forms are appear in many different alphabets, where they represent quite different phonetic sounds, or different concepts. However, because each of them in their own way is related to the function of the human organism, the magical and transformative aspects of characters and sigils are not restricted to, one system, and can be attained through the use of any of the ancient alphabet-systems of the west.

In esoteric terms, all archaic sigils have a magical and religious significance. This is especially true of writing. Several European legends explain the otherworldly nature through myths that tell how they came into the world of humans by supernatural means. Thus, a many myths tell how human beings received alphabetical letters from divine sources. According to one Greek legend, it was Hermes, the god of the crossroads, travel, commerce and writing who invented letters when he saw a flock of cranes flying through the sky. The

---

Fig. 50. The author's illuminated manuscript of the extended rune row.

different forms they made evoked the concept that characters could be arranged to represent sounds. Another origin-myth, which appears to be the most accurate historically, states that the Greek alphabet was invented by Cadmus the Phoenician, founder of the Greek city of Thebes according to classical rites. The Phoenician alphabet was the starting-point for both the Hebrew and Greek alphabets. The Greek alphabet was developed during the middle of the eighth century BCE, and, later, the Etruscan, Runic and Latin alphabets emerged from it. Many of the early Greek characters are very close to archaic Phoenician forms, and it is possible that the Greeks learnt the script from Phoenician traders who had settled in such strategically-important places as Cos, Crete and Rhodes.

A further interpretation of the origin of letters is recorded by Caius Julius Hyginus, who was the curator of the Palatine Library in Rome and a friend of the poet Ovid. In his *Fables*, he wrote that the Greek alphabet was arrived at by a process of accretion. In the first instance, the Fates themselves invented the first seven characters. These were Alpha, Beta, Eta, Ypsilon, Iota, Omicron and Tau. After this, Palamedes, son of Nauplius, invented eleven more. Then Epicharmus of Sicily added Theta and Chi (alternatively Pi and Psi). Finally, Simonides contributed the letters Omega, Epsilon, Zeta and Psi (or Phi) to the alphabet.

According to Celtic tradition, the mystical basis of the Ogham system of writing, used mainly in the British Isles, is in the trees. But it was discovered by a divine being. In the Irish language spoken to-day, the word *Ogham* naturally means the ancient alphabet. But the related word *oghum* in the Scottish Gaelic language refers to the occult sciences. Also, the Irish name of the month of June, in which the summer solstice falls, is *Ogmhios,* for the name Ogma is associated with an old Irish solar deity, appropriate for one who brings illumination. The fifteenth-century Irish manuscript called *The Book of Ballymote*, which is the main source of information on traditional Ogham, described the origin of the *Ogaim na nGadhel*, the Irish Oghams. In the question-and-answer method typical of Druidic teaching methods, it asks:

"From whence, what time, and what person, and from what cause did the ogham spring?" It answers, "The place is Hybernia's Isle, which we Scots inhabit; in the time of Breass, the son of Elathan, then king of all Ireland. The person was Ogma, MacElathan, the son of Dealbadh, brother to Breass; for Breass, Ogma and Dealbadh were three sons of Elathan, who was he son of Dealbath."

The originator of Ogham, like Odin, discoverer of the runes, was one of three brothers, recalling the triadic order of things so common in the Northern Tradition.

"Ogma, being a man much skilled in dialects and in poetry", continues *The Book of Ballymote*, "it was he who invented ogham, its object being for signs of secret speech known only to the learned, and designed to be kept from the vulgar and poor of the nation...It is called ogham, from the inventor, Ogma. The derivation is ogham, from 'ghuaim', that is the 'guaim' or wisdom through which the bards were enabled to compose; for by its branches the Irish Bards sounded their verses. "Soim" was the first thing written in ogham. On a Birch it was written, and given to Lugh, the son of Etlem....".

The means of writing in Ogham is unlike any other western alphabet. Instead of being written in separate characters, either individually or cursively, the Ogham sigils are drawn out along a line. This is the 'principal ridge' or 'stem line', which is known as the *druim*, which can represent a ridge of hills, or the edge of a wooden stave. Each Ogham character must be in contact with this line, being scribed above, below or through it. Conventionally, Ogham inscriptions were generally written vertically, starting below in Abred and ascending the cosmic axis towards Gwynvyd. When Oghams are written horizontally, as on a few ancient artifacts, the upper side of the druim is always taken to be the left-hand side, and beneath it, the right-

174

hand side. Conceptually, then, the ogham script is written from left to right. When Oghams are scribed on a standing stone, they are made across the corner between flat surfaces, known as the arris. On stone, the vowels are formed sometimes by indentations or dots.

The Book of Ballymote explains the basic form and derivation of the oghams: "From whence come the figures and names in the explanation of B, L and N ogham? From the branches and limbs of the Oak Tree: they formed ideas which they expressed in sounds, that is, as the stalk of the bush is its noblest part, from them they formed the seven chief figures as vowels, thus: A, O, U, E, I, EA, OI......and they formed three others, which they added to these as helpers, formed on different sides of the line, thus: UI, IA, AE....The branches of the wood give figures for the branches and veins of ogham, chief of all. The tribe of B from Birch, and the daughter, that is the ash of the wood, is chief; and of them the first alphabet was formed; of L, from Luis, the Quicken Tree of the wood; F from Fearn, the Alder, good for shields; S from Sail, a Willow from the wood; N in ogham from Nin, the Ash for spears; H from Huath, Whitethorn, a crooked tree or bush, because of her thorns; D from Dur, the oak of Fate from the wood; T from Tine, Cypress, or from the Elder Tree; C from Coll, the Hazel of the wood; Q from Quert, Apple, Aspen or Mountain Ash; M from Mediu, the Vine, branching finely; G from Gort, Ivy towering; NG from Ngetal or Gilcach, a Reed; ST or Z from Draighean, Blackthorn; R, Graif [not explained here]; A from Ailm, Fir; O from On, the Broom or Furze; U from Up, Heath; E from Edadh, trembling Aspen; I from Ida or Ioda, the Yew tree; EA, Eabhadh, the Aspen; OI, Oir, the Spindle Tree; UI, Uinlleann, Honeysuckle; IO, Ifin, the Gooseberry; AE,

---

Fig. 51. Versions of the Welsh *Coelbren* used by Druids and Bards. 1 - 3. Ancient *coelbren* rows from manuscripts rescued by Llewellyn Sion from Rhaglan Castle; 4 and 5. Two rows used by the bard Meurig Dafydd.

175

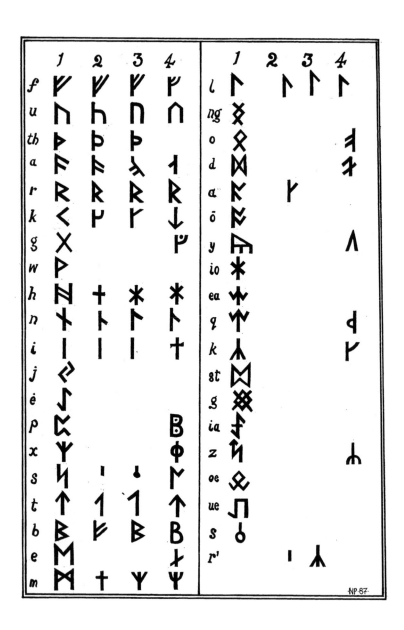

Amancholl, the Witch Hazel; Pine Ogham, that is the divine Pine from the wood, from whence are drawn the four 'Ifins', or Vineyard, thus #, *per alios*, the name of that branch."

Like other European sacred and magical alphabets, the letters of the Welsh Bardic alphabet known as *Coelbren y Beirdd* are held to encapsulate the basic structure of being.

Also, as with other alphabet-origin myths the genesis of the Bardic Coelbren is ascribed to the divine. In British Druidic teaching, letters originated simultaneously with the creation of material existence, coming into being as an integral function of the Name of God. According to a text in *Barddas*: "When God pronounced his name, with the word sprang the light and the life, for previously, there was no life but God himself. And the way it was spoken was of God's direction. His name was pronounced, and with the utterance was the springing of light and vitality, and man, and every other living thing; that is to say, each and all sprang together."

Thus, the British Druids see the creation of all things in terms of a primal vibration, which according to the Celtic Christian interpretation is the Word of God. From the light, the most perfect manifestation of the divine, came the revelation of the concept of writing:

"Menw Hen ap y Menwyd (Menw the Aged, son of Menwyd)", *Barddas* tells us, "beheld the springing of the light, and its form and appearance.... in three columns; and in the rays of light, the vocalisation - for one were the hearing and seeing, one in unison with the form and sound was life, and one unitedly with

Fig. 52. The major runic systems. 1. The Elder Futhark and additions; 2. Runes from a memorial stone at Rök in Sweden, c. 850 CE; 3. Danish 'mixed' runes; 4. 'Dotted runes' or *Alphabetum Gothicum*, Sweden.

these three was power, which power was God the Father. And by seeing the form, and in it hearing the voice - not otherwise - he knew what form and appearance voice should have...And it was on hearing the sound of the voice, which had in it the kind and utterance of three notes, that he obtained the three letters, and knew the sign that was suitable to one and other of them. Thus he made in form and sign the Name of God, after the semblance of rays of light, and perceived that they were the figure and form and sign of life.....It was from the understanding thus obtained in respect of this voice, that he was able to assimilate mutually every other voice as to kind, quality and reason, and could make a letter suitable to the utterance of every sound and voice. Thus were obtained the Cymraeg, and every other language."

As in the Jewish tradition, the Druidic Holy Name of God, from which all things were held to emanate, was rarely uttered for respect and fear of the consequences. However, "It is considered presumptuous to utter this name in the hearing of any man in the world. Nevertheless, every thing calls him inwardly by this name - the sea and land, earth and air, and all the visibles and invisibles of the world, whether on the earth or in the sky - all the worlds of all of the celestials and the terrestrials - every intellectual being and existence..."

The ancient British Name of God was symbolised by the Awen, a sigil written as three lines that radiate from above. This sigil may be compared directly with the Jewish 'tetragrammaton', the four Hebrew letters that embody the name and power of creation. In the British tradition, wach of the three lines of the Awen has a specific meaning and significance: "Thus are they made", *Barddas* recounts, " - the first of the signs is a small cutting or line inclining with the sun at eventide, thus /; the second is another cutting, in the form of a perpendicular, upright post, I; and the third is a cutting of the same amount of inclination as the first, but in an opposite direction, that is, against the sun, thus \; and the three placed together, thus /I\."
The Awen thereby symbolises the threefold or triadic nature of

all things. Curiously, this symbol is still used today, but in the guise of the 'broad arrow' that denotes British Government property, and the mark-points from which the Ordnance Survey measured the land of Britain. In its proper usage, it was the bardic symbol for wisdom, and hence remains the primary sigil of modern Druidism. The Awen may also be expressed in the alternative alphabetical form of OIV, which is even closer to the concept of the Tetragrammaton, but retains its triadic structure according to Bardic custom. According to tradition, the meaning of the character O signifies the first column of light. The second letter, I, refers to the second or middle light-column, and the third character, V, signifies the third column. *Barddas* informs us that the 'word' is significant because "it was by means of this word that God declared his existence, life, knowledge, power, eternity and universality. And in the declaration was his love, that is coinstantaneously with it sprung like lightning all the universe into life and existence, co-vocally and co-jubilantly with the uttered Name of God, in one united song of exultation and joy - then all the worlds to the extremities of Annwn".

Related to the Druidic Awen is the Valknut, a Northern Tradition sigil which is constructed from three interlinked equilateral triangles. Most basically, these three triangles signify the triadic nature of existence, as exemplified in the three main levels of the cosmic axis, below, here and above. The name Valknut denotes 'the knot of the fallen', those who are the chosen ones of Valhalla, the exceptional warriors who, having died heroically in battle, have proved themselves worthy representatives of the gods. Occasionally, the Valknut is depicted with an eye at the centre. Derived from Masonic tradition, where the eye of God appears within the triangle of the Trinity, the eye-Valknut denotes the single, yet all-seeing, eye of Odin.

But the Valknut proper is made from three distinct triangles, They are interlaced with one another in an ingenious form whose structure guarantees that each of the three triangles comes into contact with the other two. Thus, there are three

combinations, and each triangle appears successively as the outer, inner and middle row of the figure. The Valknut is thus emblematical of the integration of three identical, yet separate, patterns or qualities. In a multivalent manner, they may denote any threefold nature that emanates from the three states of time, past, present and future. Traditionally, these states are expressed as the three Norns - Urd, Verdandi and Skuld. This threefold symbol also refers to the three planes of existence inherent in the cosmic axis: the underworld, Annwn; the middle world Abred and the upper world, Gwynvyd. Another interpretation sees the three triangles as signifying the theory of the three states of the human being: body, spirit and soul. In its geometry, the Valknut is composed of nine separate lines, which can be seen to represent the nine worlds of Norse cosmology, and the wiccan 'power of three times three'. Thus, magically, like the Druidic Awen, the power of the Valknut invokes the essential eternal unity of space and time.

Another, less-recognised European system of spirituality is found in Gypsy tradition. Generally, the Romani signs and letters are called Patrin, sometimes spelt Patran, which means "a leaf of a tree". Traditional Romani signs use natural materials: leaves, sticks, rags, ashes from fires, etc. The signs can be made to impart information or news to other Romani who may pass by. They are laid at crossroads to show others the direction that the family or tribe has taken; they can also denote births, marriages and deaths. For instance, a birth is marked by tying an elder branch to a tree. If white thread is used, the baby is a girl; if red thread, a boy. Sometimes the sign

---

Fig. 53. Aspects of the runes. Top left: The Swedish alphabetic runes, called *Alphabetum Gothicum*, 1500s. Top right: A Pagan shrine with standing stones and runic trilithon guarding the sacred flame. Middle: Notation of the days of the year, from a Runestock or Clog Almanac; Below left: The Valknut; middle: Anglo-Saxon Valknut ring from Peterborough; right: Runic notation from a Swedish printed calendar of 1744.

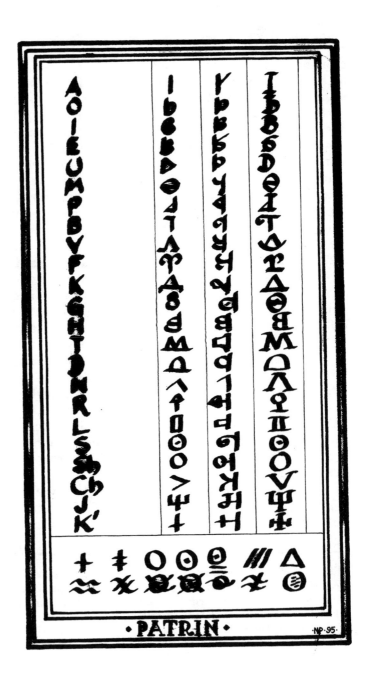

·PATRIN·

·NP·95·

182

of the particular tribe is made. This can also be a certain type of branch. It is traditional for the 'chief' or 'king' of the tribe to carry the tribal sign inside his rod of office. When he is inaugurated, he slices his staff down the middle and carves the sign upon the flat surface. It is then bound up again, thereby concealing the sign within the staff. Patrin patterns are also embroidered on clothes, hammered into metalwork and painted on vehicles and other possessions. Romani Patrin has an undefined number of sigils used to tell others certain vital information, such as how the Gorgio receive Romani visitors. These are simple graffiti, customarily made in the dust of the roadside or chalked on gateposts and doors.

There is also a Romani alphabet, recorded by the Romani scholar J-A. Decourdemanche in 1908 in his *Grammaire du Tchingan" ou langue des Bohémiens errants*, which is said to have resemblances to Magyar and Turkic 'runes'. The Romani alphabet has three forms: an alphabet for children, *c'avorengera kripta*; one for men, *rumengera kripta*; and one for the elders and the dead, *purengora kripta*. Each version of the Romani alphabet has 23 characters, 5 vowels and 18 consonants. Like the letters of the Greek alphabet, the Germanic Runes and the Celtic Oghams, each Romani character has a meaning.

Fig. 54. Patrin, Gypsy signs and alphabets. Left vertical row: *c'avorengera kripta*, the children's aphabet; Second row: *rumengera kripta*, the men's alphabet; Right row: *purengera kripta*, the alphabet of the Elders and the dead. Below, top line: 1. Here they give nothing; 2. Beggars are badly treated here; 3. Generous people here; 4. Very generous people, friendly to Romani, live here; 5. We are regarded as thieves here; 5. We have already robbed this place; 6. The people here are amenable to having their fortunes told. Lower line: 1. The mistress of the house wants a child; 2. The mistress of the house wants no more children; 3. An old woman died recently here; 4. An old man died here recently; 5. The mistress of the house likes to dally with men; 6. The master of the house likes to dally with women; 7. There is a dispute over an inheritance here.

The five vowels, which are considered separate, carry the core values of the tradition, resembling the five elements of the Druidic system described elsewhere in this book. The form of the vowel A, which represents the element earth, signifies the ground, a place or habitation. It has the sexual meaning of a eunuch. The letter O, which corresponds with the element of fire, stands for strength in the sense of force, heat and light. Sexually, it signifies the phallus. The character I corresponds with the element of water, standing for liquidness and mucosity. It symbolises the vulva. The letter E stands for the quality of being and the presence of existence as a thing. It signifies the union of the male and female, the phallus in the vulva. The final vowel, U, represents sound in the form of a cry, a voice or noise. It signifies the absence of sex.

The eighteen consonants have the following order: M, P, B, V, F, K, G, H, T, D, N, R, L, S, Sh, Ch, J, K. M stands for *mui,* and means 'mouth'. Its form in the children's and elders' alphabet resembles a mouth. P, *pai,* a foot, is also pictographic in form. The stick-like letter *bai,* the letter B, means a stick or rod; whilst *vai,* the letter V, looks like walking legs and means a traveller. F stands for *fai,* a well, spring or fountain, whose spouting waters the letter resembles. It is also close to representations of Irminsul. The letter K, *ker,* which means 'tent', resembles the simple tents used by the Romani in the days before horse-drawn and motorised caravans. G, *gon* means a purse, whilst H stands for *herko* a bow, whose form resembles the bows used by the Turkic warriors of old. The letter T, *tem,* the earth, resembles the double-mountain breast of Mother Earth, or the axe, whilst D, *dom* is the 'house', in the form of a bender-tent. The character corresponding with N is *nak,* the nose, whilst R is *ruk* a tree. L stands for *lir* a pound or enclosure in which horses and other livestock are kept. S, *sin,* signifies a star by a point within a circle for the children's and elders' alphabets, whilst Sh is *s'on,* the moon. It is represented by an empty circle. The pointed letter that means Ch is *c'ok,* the beak. J is represented by *jine* a person, whilst the final letter, K is *k'ando,* a sword.

Although the Romani alphabet is less well known than the Runes or Oghams, it is an important example of the tradition where letters were derived from pictograms of the individual things most important to members of society. Like in the Norse text *Alvismal,* where the dwarf Alvis tells the Asa-Thor the names of the 13 most important things in the world according to men, gods, giants and dwarves, the Romani alphabet uses different characters to depict existence according to, *c'avorengera kripta; rumengera kripta*; and *purengora kripta.* According to Alvis, there are 52 descriptions, 13 things seen from four different world-world-views. This is a classical way of looking at the world, best known in the traditional four elements of European spirituality, and the four suits of the Tarot deck. According to Alvis, the world is seen in the following way:

	Humans	Gods	Giants	Dwarves
1. Earth	earth	fields and ways	evergreen place	clay, growing place
2. Heaven	heaven	warmer of the heights	the wind weaver	high home, fair roof
3. The Moon	moon	mock sun	night traveller	month-shower, whirling wheel
4. Sun	sun, Sol	shining orb	ever bright	fair wheel, Dvalin's delight
5. Wind	wind	noise-maker	wailer	roaring traveller
6. Calm	calm	quietness	wind's husk	day's refuge
7. Clouds	sky	shower bringers	wind-floes	rain-bearers, helmets of darkness
8. Ocean	sea	home of waves	home of eels	the big drink, the deep
9. Fire	fire	flamer	greedy one	burner, furnace, destroyer
10. Wood	wood	shelter of the fields	fuel	adorner of the hills, fair limbs
11. Seed	barley	grain, grower	food maker	maker of slender stalks
12. Ale	beer	foamer	swill	good cheer, mead
13. Night	night	darkness	day's mask	unlight, bringer of dreams.

Contemporary studies into the nature of human perception may provide us with another possibility of understanding the meaning of sigils, one embedded deeply within our own human consciousness. Neurophysiologists have described certain geometrical shapes and images that they believe to occur in the visual cortex and neural system of each human being. These subconscious images they call 'phosphenes' are said to be 'entopic', that is, they are visible with shut eyes. The phosphenes can also appear in the consciousness when the brain's state is altered by some means from its normal condition. This may take place during prayer, meditation or contemplation; in states of trance; or during periods of delirium induced by fatigue, illness, disease or artificial stimulants. People experiencing such abnormal states, frequently 'see' entopic geometric shapes which are sometimes closely related to alphabetic characters. These altered states of consciousness are sought by those who voluntarily walk the thin line between life and death in search of enlightenment, the witch, the magician, the shaman and the religious ecstatic. In Norse mythology, Odin's discovery of the runes comes through his self-inflicted ordeal of fatigue and agony on the cosmic axis, the 'windswept tree'.

By means of such esoteric techniques, some life-threateningly dangerous and less altered and novel states of consciousness can be achieved, through which, hopefully, new insights can be obtained. But, necessarily, in order that they can be transmitted to other human beings at all, these insights must appear within a format which coincides with the innate structure of human consciousness. If we accept the phosphene theory, then the myth of Odin's inner rune-quest is a perfect tale of the conscious realisation and ordering of these inherent phosphene patterns. According to this view, which is not incompatible with the symbolic, sacred mythos, external symbols and sacred alphabets are a real way reflections of the internal neurophysiological constitution of human beings. Simultaneously, they are also metaphorical presentations of external reality.

Postscript

The greater the understanding of the meaning of signs, sigils and symbols, the greater the danger that they will be misused. In modern times, the advertising business is an example of how the psychoanalytical work of Sigmund Freud and others has been used to make the public buy products. Similarly, the appropriation of the swastika by Hitlerism has shown how an ancient and venerable sigil can be taken over and effectively altered. Likewise, the insights of C.G. Jung and Joseph Campbell among others are the underlying groundbase of many a Hollywood film or music video. However, although these and other widespread examples of the modern 'unspirit' appear to be dominant in contemporary society, they have not entirely prevented individuals from having direct experiences of the symbolic world. The inner structure of the human being and the physical nature of existence outside has not changed: our perception is still that of our ancestors, that the elements we recognise as consciousness and spirit are diffused throughout the cosmos. They are present everywhere, and, as there is no definite boundary between individual human beings and the outer world, both in space and time, the ancient correspondence between microcosm and macrocosm remains unbroken.

This ancient reality, formulated by Hermes Trismegistus, has empowered human culture throughout history. In those ages when the Hermetic Maxim has been the conscious groundbase of human culture, which is the greater part of western civilisation, the understanding has been life-enriching. At the present day, this archaic realisation is still a reality, despite

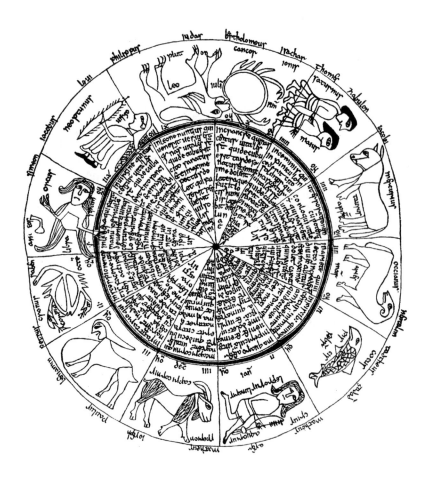

being distorted and marginalised by the material and organisational demands of industrial society. But it is clearly evident that the present age is in need of a much more widespread understanding of those exquisitely fine perceptions which were accepted as normal, indeed essential, by the sages of old. When we apply ancient skills and wisdom to present conditions, we can cross the barriers between the worlds, and bring the hidden, unconscious possibilities of existence into the realm of consciousness. Not to do so is to deny our human birthright, the exercise of awareness. Only to do so is to be truly human.

Fig. 55. A medieval Irish zodiac, symbol of wholeness, completion and new beginnings.

Bibliography

Ab Ithell, J. Williams: Barddas; or, a Collection of Original Documents, illustrative of the Theology, Wisdom and Usages of the Bardo-Druidic System of the Isle of Britain. 2 vols.,The Welsh Mss. Society, Llandovery, 1862.

Agrell, Sigurd: Semantik Mysterierreligion och nordisk Runmagi. Bonniers, Stockholm, 1931.

Anonymous: The Bonesman's Bible, English manuscript, n.d.

Aswynn, Freya: Leaves of Yggdrassil. Privately Published, London, 1988.

Awolalu, J.O.: Yoruba Beliefs and Sacrificial Rites. Longmans, London, 1979.

Barker, W.H. and Sinclair, Cecilia: West African Folk-Tales. Harrap, London, 1917.

Bascom, William R.: Ifa Divination. Communication Between Gods and Men in West Africa. Indiana University Press, Bloomington, 1969.

Bascom, William R.: Sixteen Cowries. Yoruba Divination from Africa to the New World. Indiana University Press, Bloomington, 1980.

Bastide, Roger: The African Religions of Brazil. Johns Hopkins University Press, Baltimore, 1978.

Binder, Peral: Magic Symbols of the World. Hamlyn, London, 1972.

Bingham, Joseph: Origines Ecclesiasticae, or, the Antiquities of the Christian Church. Robert Knaplock, London, 1708.

Behm, Jacob (Jacob Böhme): Four Tables of Divine Revelation. H. Blunden, London, 1654.

Bucknell, Peter A.: Entertainment and Ritual 600 - 1600. Stainer & Bell, London, 1979.

Burland, C.A.: The Arts of the Alchemists. Wiedenfeld and Nicolson, London, 1967.

Butler, Bill: The Definitive Tarot. Century, London, 1975.

Campion, Nicholas: An Introduction to the History of Astrology. ISCWA, London, 1982.

Charters, Samuel: Robert Johnson. Oak Publications, New York, 1973.

Christian, Roy: Old English Customs. David & Charles, Newton Abbot, 1974.

Cooper, J.C.: The Aquarian Dictionary of Festivals. Aquarian, London, 1990.

Courlander, Harold: Tales of Yoruba Gods and Heroes. Crown Publishers, New York, 1973.

Cyr, Donald (ed.): Celtic Secrets. Stonehenge Viewpoint. Santa Barbara, 1990.

Cyr, Donald (ed.): The Crystal Veil. Avant-Garde Archaeology. Stonehenge Viewpoint, Santa Barbara, 1995.

Davies, Glenys (ed.): Polytheistic Systems. Cosmos Yearbook. Traditional Cosmology Society, Edinburgh, 1989.

Deren, Maya: Divine Horsemen. Thames and Hudson, London, 1953.

Drake-Carnell, F. J.: Old English Customs and Ceremonies. Batsford, London, 1938.

Elworthy, Frederick Thomas: The Evil Eye. John Murray, London, 1895.

Evans-Wentz, W.Y.: The Fairy Faith in Celtic Countries. Oxford University Press, Oxford, 1911.

Fabelo, T.D.: Lengua de Santeros. Editorial Adelante, Havana, 1956.

Fabricius, Johannes: Alchemy - The Medieval Alchemists and Their Royal Art. Rosenkilde & Bagger, KØbenhavn, 1976.

Flowers, Stephen: Runes and Magic: Magical Formulaic Elements in the Older Runic Tradition. Lang, New York, 1986.

Flowers, Stephen: The Galdrabök: An Icelandic Grimoire. Samuel Weiser, York Beach, 1989.

Foster, Richard: Patterns of Thought, the Hidden Meaning of the Great Pavement at Westminster Abbey. Cape, London, 1991.

Gansohr, Heidi and Döring, Alois: Kirchturmhöhne. Rheinland-Verlag, Köln, 1984.

Gettings, Fred: Dictionary of Occult, Hermetica and Alchemical Signs. Routledge and Kegan Paul, London, 1981.

Gleason, Judith: A Recitation of Ifa, Oracle of the Yoruba. Grossmann, New York, 1973.

Gonzalez-Wippler, Migene: Santeria, African Magic in Latin America. Original, New York, 1984.

Gorsleben, Rudolf J.: Die Hoch-Zeit der Menschheit. Köhler und Amerlang, Leipzig, 1930.

Grant, Kenneth: Images and Oracle of Austin Osman Spare. Frederick Muller, London, 1975.

Grant, Kenneth: Cults of the Shadow. Frederick Muller, London, 1975.

Green, Martin: Curious Customs. Impact Books, London, 1993.

Gundarsson, Kvedúlfr Hagan (ed.): Our Troth, by thne Ring of Troth and Other True Folk. The Ring of Troth, 1993.

Hancox, Joy: The Byrom Collection, Cape, London, 1992.

Hartley, Christine: The Western Mystery Tradition. Aquarian, London, 1968.

Herrmann, Paul: Das altgermanische Priesterwesen. Diderichs, Jena, 1929.

Hobbs, J. Walter: Masonic Ritual. Described, Compared and Explained. The Masonic Record Co., London, 1923.

Horst, Georg Conrad: Zauber-Bibliothek oder von Zauberei, Theurgie und Mantik, Gespenstern und Geistererscheinungen. Kupferberg, Mainz, 1821.

Howes, Michael: Amulets. Robert Hale, London, 1975.

Huxley, F.: The Way of the Sacred. Thames and Hudson, London, 1974.

Jencks, Charles: Towards a Symbolic Architecture: The Thematic House. Rizzoli, New York, 1985.

Jensen, K. Frank: The Prophetic Cards - a catalog of fortune-telling cards. (Vol 1) Oroboros, Roskilde, 1985.

Jensen, K. Frank: The Prophetic Cards - a catalog of fortune-telling cards. (Vol. 2) Oroboros, Roskilde, 1990.

Johfra: Astrology. V.O.C. Angel Books, Amsterdam, 1981.

Johnson, Robert: Delta Blues Legend. Charly Blues Masterworks No. 13. (2 Compact Discs), London, 1992.

Jones, Bernard E.: Freemasons' Guide and Compendium. Harrap, London, 1950.

Jones, Prudence: Eight and Nine: Sacred Numbers of Sun and Moon in the Pagan North. Fenris-Wolf, Bar Hill, 1982.

Jones, Prudence: Sundial and Compass Rose: Eight-fold Time Division in Northern Europe. Fenris-Wolf, Bar Hill, 1982.

Jones, Prudence: A 'House' System From Viking Europe. Fenris-Wolf, Cambridge, 1991.

Jones, Prudence: Northern Myths of the Constellations. Fenris-Wolf, Cambridge, 1991.

Jones, Prudence (ed.): Creative Astrology. Aquarian Press, London, 1991.

Jones, Prudence and Pennick, Nigel: A History of Pagan Europe. Routledge, London, 1995.

Jung, Carl Gustav: Man and His Symbols. Aldus, London, 1964.

Jung, Carl Gustav: Mysterium Coniunctionis. Princeton University Press, New York, 1970.

Jung, Carl Gustav: Psychology and Alchemy. Princeton University Press, New York, 1970.

Jung, Carl Gustav: The Archetypes and the Collective Unconscious. Routledge and Kegan Paul, London, 1971.

Kaplan, Stuart J.: Encyclopedia of Tarot, 3 vols. U.S. Games Systems, New York, 1978, 1985 and 1986.

Kern, Hermann: Labyrinthe. Prestel-Verlag, München, 1982.

Knappert, Jan: African Mythology. Diamond Books, London, 1995.

Lachatanere, Romulu: Manuel de Santeria. Caribe, Havana, 1942.

Le Corbusier: The Modulor: A Harmonious Measure to the Human Scale Universally Applicable to Architecture and Mechanics. Faber and Faber, London, 1954.

Lévi, Eliphas: The History of Magic. Rider, London, 1971.

Lévi, Eliphas: Transcendental Magic: Rider, London, 1972.

Levis, Howard C.: Bladud of Bath. West Country Editions, Bath, 1973.

Lister, Raymond: Decorative Cast Ironwork in Great Britain. Bell, London, 1960.

Longworth, T. Clifton: The Worship of Love: A Study of Nature Worship Throughout the World. Torchstream Books, London, 1954.

MacKay, Charles: Memoirs of Extraordinary Popular Delusions and the Madness of Crowds. The National Illustrated :Library, London, 1852.

Mann, A.T.: The Round Art. The Astrology of Time and Space. Dragon's World, London, 1979.

Maple, Eric: Deathly Magic. Thorsons, Wellingborough, 1976.

Mathers, S.L. MacGregor: The Book of the Sacred Magic of Abra-Melin the Mage. Thorsons, Wellingborough, 1976.

atthews, John (ed.): The World Atlas of Divination. Eddison-Sadd Editions, London, 1992.

Michell, John: City of Revelation, Garnstone Press, London, 1972.

Michell, John: Simulacra. Thames and Hudson, London, 1979.

Michell, John: At the Centre of the World. Polar Symbolism Discovered in Celtic, Norse and Other Ritualized Landscapes. Thames and Hudson, London, 1994.

Mockridge, Patricia, and Mockridge, Philip: Weathervanes of Great Britain. Robert Hale, London, 1990.

Mowl, Tim and Earnshaw, Brian: John Wood: Architect of Obsession. Millstream Books, Bath, 1988.

Muchery, Georges: The Astrological Tarot. Bracken Books, London, 1989.

Nasr, Seyyed Hossein: Islamic Science. World Of Islam Festival Publishing, Teheran, 1976.

Nataf, André: The Wordsworth Dictionary of the Occult. Wordsworth Reference, Ware, 1994.

Nichols, Ross: The Book of Druidry. Aquarian, London, 1990.

O'Brien, Flann: The Third Policeman. MacGibbon and Kee, London, 1967.

Owen, A.L.: The Famous Druids: A Survey of Three Centuries of English Literature on Druids. Oxford University Press, Oxford, 1962.

Pagdin, W.E.: The Story of the Weathercock. Edward Appleby, Stockton-on-Tees, 1949.

Pálsson, Einar: Evil and the Earth:. The Symbolic Background of Mör\r Valgar\ sson in Njals Saga. Mimir, Reykjavik, 1993.

Pálsson, Einar: The Sacred Triangle of Pagan Iceland. Mimir, Reykjavik, 1993.

Parrinder, E.G.: Witchcraft, European and African. Faber and Faber, London, 1963.

Pennick, Nigel: The Mysteries of King's College Chapel. Cockaygne, Cambridge, 1974.

Pennick, Nigel: Madagascar Divination. Fenris-Wolf, Bar Hill, 1976.

Pennick, Nigel: The Swastika. Fenris-Wolf, Bar Hill, 1979.

Pennick, Nigel: The Ancient Science of Geomancy. Thames & Hudson, London, 1979.

Pennick, Nigel: The Subterranean Kingdom. Turnstone, Wellingborough, 1981.

Pennick, Nigel: Earth Harmony. Siting and Protecting Your Home: A Practical and Spiritual Guide. Century, London, 1987.

Pennick, Nigel: The Cosmic Axis. Runestaff, Bar Hill, 1987.

Pennick, Nigel: Landscape Lines, Leys and Limits in Old England. Runestaff, Bar Hill, 1987.

Pennick, Nigel: Einst War Uns Die Erde Helig. Felicitas-Hübner Verlag, Waldeck-Dehringhausen, 1987.

Pennick, Nigel: Lost Lands and Sunken Cities. Fortean Tomes, London, 1987.

Pennick, Nigel: Traditional Board Games of Northern Europe. Valknut Productions, Bar Hill, 1988.

Pennick, Nigel: Mazes and Labyrinths. Robert Hale, London, 1990.

Pennick, Nigel: Das Runen Orakel. Droemer Knaur, München, 1990.

Pennick, Nigel: Secret Games of the Gods. Weiser, York Beach, 1992.

Pennick, Nigel: The Pagan Book of Days. Destiny, Rochester, Vermont, 1992.

Pennick, Nigel: Rune Magic. Aquarian, London, 1992.

Pennick, Nigel: Celtic Art in the Northern Tradition. Nideck, Bar Hill, 1992.

Pennick, Nigel: Visions of the Goddess. Nideck, Bar Hill, 1993.

Pennick, Nigel: Anima Loci. Nideck, Bar Hill, 1993.

Pennick, Nigel: Practical Magic in the Northern Tradition. Thoth, Loughborough, 1994.

Pennick, Nigel: Sacred Geometry. Capall Bann, Chieveley, 1994.

Pennick, Nigel: Σο Δoε Τησ. Diipetes, Athens, 1994.

Pennick, Nigel: The Oracle, of Geomancy. Capall Bann, Chieveley, 1995.

Pennick, Nigel: Runic Astrology. Capall Bann, Chieveley, 1995.

Pennick, Nigel: The Inner Mysteries of the Goths. Capall Bann, Chieveley, 1995

Pennick, Nigel: Secrets of East Anglian Magic. Robert Hale, London, 1995.

Petrie, Flinders: Decorative Patterns of the Ancient World. Studio, London, 1930.

Rackham, Oliver: The History of the Countryside. J.M. Dent and Sons, London, 1986.

Rand, Harry: Hundertwasser. Benedikt Taschen Verlag, Köln, 1991.

Rees, Alwyn, and Rees, Brinley: Celtic Heritage. Thames and Hudson, London, 1967.

Reuter, Otto Sigfrid: Germanische Himmelskunde. Köhler und Amerlang, Leipzig, 1929.

Reuter, Otto Sigfrid: Skylore of the North. Runestaff, Bar Hill, 1985.

Rimmer, Alfred: Ancient Stone Crosses of England. Virtue, Spalding and Co., London, 1875.

Roberts, Anthony: Atlantean Traditions in Ancient Britain. Unicorn, Llanfynydd, 1974.

Robertson, Olivia: The Call of Isis. Cesara Publications, Enniscorthy, 1975.

Screeton, Paul: The Labton Worm and Other Northumbrian Dragon Legends. Zodiac House, London, 1978.

Shah, Idries: The Secret Lore of Magic. Sphere Books, London, 1972.

Stewart, Cecil: Gothic Architecture.Longmans, London, 1961.

Stirling, William: The Canon: An Exposition of the Pagan Mystery Perpetuated in the Cabala as the Rule of All the Arts. Garnstone Press, London, 1974.

Storms, G.: Anglo-Saxon Magic. Nijhoff, Den Haag, 1948.

Stretton, Clement E.: Tectonic Art: Ancient Trade Guilds and Companies. Melton Mowbray Times Company, Melton Mowbray, 1909.

Stuart, Alec: The Septiform System of the Cosmos. Jarrold, Norwich, 1932.

Stubbes, Thomas: The Anatomy of Abuses, London, 1583.

Suster, Gerald: The Truth About the Tarot. Skoob Books Publishing, London, 1990.

Svendsen, Peter Juhl: Rundetarn Opklaret: Katedralens Mysterium. Sphinx, KØbenhavn, 1987.

Tauxier, L.: Le Noir du Yatenga. Emile Larose, Paris, 1917.

Tempels, P.: Bantu Philosophy. Presence Africaine, Paris, 1959.

Thomas, Patrick: Candle in the Darkness: Celtic Spirituality from Wales. Gomer, Llandysul, 1993.

Timmers, J.J.M.: A Handbook of Romanesque Art. Nelson, London, 1969.

Tolkien, J.R.R.: Tree and Leaf. George Allen and Unwin, London, 1964.

Valiente, Doreen: Natural Magic. Robert Hale, London, 1975.

Van Serima, Ivan, ed.: Black Women in Antiquity. Transaction Books, London, 1988.

Von Reichenbach,Karl: The Odic Forec. University Books, New York, 1968.

Von Zaborsky, Oskar: UrvUater-Erbe in deutsches Volkskunst. Deutscher Ahnenerbe, Leipzig, 1936.

Waite, Arthur Edward: The Holy Grail: Its Legends and Symbolism. Rider, London, 1933.

Warburg, A.: Heidnisch-Antike Weissagung in Wort und Bild zu Luthers Zeiten. Carl Winter Verlag, Heideberg, 1920.

Waterfield, Robin: Jacob Boehme. Essential Readings. Crucible, Wellingborough, 1989.

Wellcome, Henry S.: Hen Feddecyaeth Kymric (Antient Cymric Medicine). Burroughs Wellcome and Co., London, Sydney and Cape Town, 1903.

Wheatley, Paul: The Pivot of the Four Quarters. Edinburgh University Press, Edinburgh, 1971.

Williams, Caroline: Saints: Their Cults and Origins. Bergstrom and Boyle, London, 1980.

Wilson, Steve: Robin Hood: The Spirit of the Forest. Neptune Press, London, 1993.

Wirth, Hermann: Die Heilige Urschrift der Menschheit. KÜhler und Amerlang, Leipzig, 1934.

Wither, George: A Collection of Emblemes, Ancient and Moderne, facsimile of the 1635 edition, Scolar Press, London, 1968.

Ziegler, Gerd: Tarot: Mirror of the Soul. Aquarian Press, Wellingborough, 1986.

Index

Other titles from Capall Bann

A detailed illustrated catalogue is available on request, SAE or International Postal Coupon appreciated. Titles are available direct from Capall Bann, post free in the UK (cheque or PO with order) or from good bookshops and specialist outlets.

Animals, Mind Body Spirit & Folklore
Angels and Goddesses - Celtic Christianity & Paganism by Michael Howard
Arthur - The Legend Unveiled by C Johnson & E Lung
Auguries and Omens - The Magical Lore of Birds by Yvonne Aburrow
Book of the Veil The by Peter Paddon
Call of the Horned Piper by Nigel Jackson
Cats' Company by Ann Walker
Celtic Lore & Druidic Ritual by Rhiannon Ryall
Compleat Vampyre - The Vampyre Shaman: Werewolves & Witchery by Nigel Jackson
Crystal Clear - A Guide to Quartz Crystal by Jennifer Dent
Earth Dance - A Year of Pagan Rituals by Jan Brodie

Earth Magic by Margaret McArthur
Enchanted Forest - The Magical Lore of Trees by Yvonne Aburrow
Healing Homes by Jennifer Dent
Herbcraft - Shamanic & Ritual Use of Herbs by Susan Lavender & Anna Franklin
In Search of Herne the Hunter by Eric Fitch
Inner Space Workbook - Developing Counselling & Magical Skills Through the Tarot
Kecks, Keddles & Kesh by Michael Bayley
Living Tarot by Ann Walker
Magical Incenses and Perfumes by Jan Brodie
Magical Lore of Animals by Yvonne Aburrow
Magical Lore of Cats by Marion Davies

Magical Lore of Herbs by Marion Davies
Masks of Misrule - The Horned God & His Cult in Europe by Nigel Jackson
Mysteries of the Runes by Michael Howard
Oracle of Geomancy by Nigel Pennick
Patchwork of Magic by Julia Day
Pathworking - A Practical Book of Guided Meditations by Pete Jennings
Pickingill Papers - The Origins of Gardnerian Wicca by Michael Howard
Psychic Animals by Dennis Bardens
Psychic Self Defence - Real Solutions by Jan Brodie
Runic Astrology by Nigel Pennick
Sacred Animals by Gordon 'The Toad' Maclellan
Sacred Grove - The Mysteries of the Forest by Yvonne Aburrow
Sacred Geometry by Nigel Pennick
Sacred Lore of Horses The by Marion Davies
Sacred Ring - Pagan Origins British Folk Festivals & Customs by Michael Howard
Secret Places of the Goddess by Philip Heselton
Talking to the Earth by Gordon Maclellan
Taming the Wolf - Full Moon Meditations by Steve Hounsome
The Goddess Year by Nigel Pennick & Helen Field
West Country Wicca by Rhiannon Ryall
Wildwood King by Philip Kane
Witches of Oz The by Matthew & Julia Phillips

Capall Bann is owned and run by people actively involved in many of the areas in which we publish. Our list is expanding rapidly so do contact us for details on the latest releases. We guarantee our mailing list will never be released to other companies or organisations.

Capall Bann Publishing, Freshfields, Chieveley, Berks, RG20 8TF.